Story Carrier

A Collection of Tales of the
Disappeared

PRAISE FOR *STORY CARRIER: A COLLECTION OF TALES OF THE DISAPPEARED*

"This wise and generous memoir takes readers on a journey to heal ancestral trauma, give voice to the silenced, and recover the mystic wonders of the Black Madonna. A journalist and a writing teacher, a daughter and a mother, Jane Clark spins a captivating tale that speaks to the heart of the mysteries hidden within all our lives. Highly recommended."

—Perdita Finn, author of *Take Back the Magic: Conversations with the Unseen World*

"Jane vividly remembers how the harsh west Texas landscape and the force of the wind have been both the culprits and resources for her story of loss, grief and transformation. Her storytelling evokes in all of us the call to recover our own stories of loss embedded in outer landscapes and to listen to the wind to become like her, a story carrier."

—Mary Aebischer PhD, Transformative Educator/ Workshop Leader

"Jane Clark's prose sings like poetry, her *Story Carrier: A Collection of Tales of the Disappeared* taking us on a journey into an emptiness as exposed and yet rich as the windy plains of West Texas, a single soul umbilically tied to persons, place, home. Jane's memoir, this soul's melody is empowered with the magic of a life traveling full circle enveloped in the black hole of dharma, female principle of the universe."

—Darlene Klein Logan, Ph.D. Former professor of Biblical Literature and English at New Mexico Military Institute and University of Texas

"*Story Carrier: A Collection of Tales of the Disappeared* by Jane Clark traces the author's unresolved grief over childhood losses through the West Texas landscape. The wind, an ever-present feature of the desert, mirrors Clark's feelings of being uprooted and blown about, but later lifts her in ways that allow her to discover her family roots and to be planted among more nuanced memories of the women in her family."

—Helen Sitler, Ph.D., Professor of English Literature and Composition Professor at Indiana University of Pennsylvania

"This memoir now written into being composes a brilliant literary endeavor spanning the distance between the haunting tones of a southern gothic childhood and the symphonic splendor of mature feminine enlightenment. Clark's remembrance carries us in seemingly effortless ways upon the white-hot flame of narrative empowerment. This work is a delicately penned expression carried with care that compels us to engage with reverence the myriad past and present experiences that compose our own stories."

—Galen Leonhardy, Professor of English Midwest Community College, Illinois. Author of *Skipping Stones: A Memoir of Teaching*

"I truly believe in the importance of this book as a guide to a collective "soul retrieval" as women who have been estranged from the ancestral women, that might offer hard-earned wisdom, examples of resiliency, inspiration, hope through their tragedies and triumphs."

—Linda Abrams, Licensed clinical social worker, founder of Alternate Roots, a center for personal and community transformation

Story Carrier

A Collection of Tales of the Disappeared

JANE CLARK

Writing Brave Press
1940 Palmer Avenue, #1032
Larchmont NY 10538
www.writingbravepress.com

Distributed by IngramSpark

Cover and Text Design: Danny Meono
Copyeditor: Meghan Muldowney
Author Photos: Samantha Wilson

Library of Congress Cataloging-in-Publication Data available.
ISBN 979-8-9873704-2-1 (paperback)
ISBN 979-8-9873704-1-4 (eBook)

First Edition

All events are written as the author recalls them, without claim that they are anything more than creations from her soul. Certain names have been changed.

This book is dedicated to:
Jeanie, Regina, and Violet Marie

STORY CARRIER:

A Collection of Tales of the Disappeared

Introduction

When I sat down to write this memoir, my desire was to tell the story of a young girl whose life had been so disrupted by loss brought about by death, divorce, and sudden moves that readers — especially parents and mental health professionals — would consider more carefully the impact of loss on young children. I would show how my mother's inability to help me cope with the sudden disappearance of half my family in one year left me in a tailspin, locking the two of us in a lifelong dance of anger and grief. I'd write about the way my hunger for a story that would explain my life led me to a career as a writer dedicated to stories about those who are silenced and who disappear.

I felt fairly confident about writing the story. After all, I held a Ph.D. in English Composition, with a specialty in Narrative Theory and Research. I had spent a dozen years teaching writing to college students, administering a writing program at a major northeastern university, and working for a national organization that led the way in changing how writing was taught in the classroom. I created and implemented a graduate curriculum program in composition, and I secured grants from the state for improving the teaching of writing across the curriculum. Before working in academia, I spent fifteen years working as a broadcast and print journalist. The one thing I felt certain of was I knew how to write a good story. So when I began to work, I thought, *I've got this.*

Very quickly, I found I'd wandered into unknown territory. The words didn't come easily, and the story seemed to take on a life of its own, twisting and turning out of my control, much like an infant struggling to get free of her mother's grasp. Over the weeks and months, I realized I was in a tug of war with a story that was overtaking me, drowning my voice. Not only could I not write it, but I wasn't sure I could find it. The story I wanted to tell was not the one that wanted to be told.

I shouldn't have been surprised. More than twenty years earlier, I stood in front of my dissertation committee arguing, "The story will always tell itself. Writers have to get out of the way and let the story unfold." I had always believed stories were alive, existing in our souls and our bodies, moving us across each day, directing our behavior much like a set of unseen operating instructions programmed into our psyches. Although I understood that story is more than an artistic construct used to frame experience in language, I did not fully understand its power. Stories seemed to know something that I did not.

Even family stories, which we think we know, become confusing when we are kept in the dark and, in some instances, lied to. They twist around one another and form knots that refuse to untangle long enough to be followed to the source.

Fifty years after my Uncle George's mysterious death, we still talked about the man who raised honeybees and chickens in his backyard in the mornings and fell onto his sofa in an intoxicated state each night, singing himself to sleep. But we never knew about the events in his life that led him to numb himself into unremembering. Perhaps even he was not aware of the stories he carried to the bottle with the setting of the sun each day. When I ran across a couple of lively characters in my ancestral line, including the notorious gunslinger Jesse James, I followed up with a genogram, complete with names, dates, and other discrete data. But not even this information was enough to pull the story of my family out of the darkness.

The truth was I'd always suspected there was an untold piece of family history hiding a relative I could never have known. For most of my life, I'd felt the weight of an unspoken hardship experienced by a descendant whose name escaped me. I sensed that something had happened to someone but I didn't know what it was or to whom it happened. At night, my sleep was disrupted by the presence of a story hovering over my soul, a piece that flashed in a colorful image or in the whisperings of an unseen person. Bits of story seemed to reach out to me in words from the lines of a poem I'd read, and in phrases heard as I eavesdropped on strangers' conversations. Pieces of story appeared and disappeared, seemingly at will, giving me a momentary glimpse of a history that quickly slipped out of my awareness. I knew I was carrying narratives that spanned generations. I just couldn't imagine what they could be.

Recent studies into the way traumatic life experiences alter gene expression suggested I was feeling the residue of events that had occurred in the lives of my ancestors. Just as we inherit family traits for height or eye color, we are bestowed with the remnants of stories carried across our lineage. I knew stories left untold in one generation would resurface in the lives of the next one, so that when a person vanished, the impression of life remained. But I also understood the dynamics of power between the story and the storyteller, which left me waiting at the threshold for a tale to appear. As folklorist Clarissa Pinkola Estes explained, stories call on us when they are ready to be told. "We are summoned by their covenant with us, not vice versa," she wrote. Still, I believed that if anyone could get her hands on a story, it would be me.

What I failed to see is that sometimes the most crucial stories of our lives have been buried in the unconscious, in what author Robert Olen Butler described as our "white hot center," the home of the imagination, alongside fantasies, myths, legends, and fairy tales. As a child, I had lived in that space in between the world of reality and the sphere of "what if," where anything was possible. My need to bring my life experience into language was so forceful that, when I was young, I confabulated tales and sometimes told lies, just to make the story appear. Looking back, I have compassion for the little girl who told fibs but did not understand that the nature of a story is to demand that we stand close to the edge of reality, at the threshold of memory and invention.

I understood the way some stories resisted being told in a linear sequence, while others were too cumbersome for the human

4

mind and they are held, as Carl Jung noted, in the collective unconscious–the large basket of tales stored in the universe. I believed some were held in place by nature, within the tissues of trees, the tiny lines on rocks, the delicate petals of flowers, the hair of the deer that run across our forests. Others were carried by the wind or buried with the remains of our ancestors. Still, I was not going to be blocked from unearthing a tale, even if it stubbornly insisted on remaining just beyond my reach.

In my search, I turned to the tales of goddesses, spiritual entities, characters in fairy tales, heroines, and mystical beings whose voices seemed to reach across time and space, offering guidance to me as I worked. Perhaps they called to me because, as Jungian psychiatrist Jean Shinoda Bolen wrote, every woman carries a life story of "mythic dimensions." I believed in the powerful patterns generated by these myths and legends that assembled themselves into archetypes, taking root in our psyches, where they had as much influence over our lives as the external cultural forces we experienced. I knew a story could inhabit my life whether I had heard it or not. I knew all this.

Years of studying stories had taught me so much. Yet, as I wrote, it became clear that I was not in control and, in spite of my knowledge about storytelling, I was unable to tell this one. Finally, it dawned on me: I was not the storyteller, I was the carrier of the story who was being taken on a journey of discovery, an unfolding of one mystery after another. In a final bid to write, I turned away from my academic training and professional experience, and allowed myself to spiral downward into the shadowy darkness of my imagination, where, as a child,

5

I had surrendered to the mystery of the unknown. I yielded to a force I didn't fully understand, trusting the story to tell itself. I got out of the way. Only then was I led to a family tale I might not have found otherwise. One of "mythic dimensions." This is a collection of tales about my somewhat erratic and, at times, terrifyingly beautiful journey, told in an unconventional, non-linear form, the way mysterious accounts about disappearing and reappearing often come into awareness.

Chapter 1

DISAPPEARED

Iraan, Texas: 1949

The room was dark, heavy drapes closed against the glaring West Texas sun. Wind rolled across the tin roof, separating panels, causing metal to scrape against metal. People I didn't know were in my house, whispering. Big people whose faces I could not see. Some gathered around my grandmother's mahogany dining table, covered with a loosely crocheted tablecloth that hung down to the floor. The one I usually climbed beneath to play hide and seek. Not today.

Cowboys took off their hats and wiped their square-toed boots at the door before walking across the room with their wives to the table where my sister's body was lying. She'd been on that table for so long. Women came with food: raisin pie, pinto beans, brisket. My grandfather pulled a flask out of his pocket and took a drink.

"I'm sorry," the strangers told my mother, hugging her and my father. No one talked to me. No one picked me up. Not today.

I was just over two years old, unable to understand why my

sister was so still and not speaking. Four years older than me, she had been the one to carry me in her arms, calling me "my baby." This morning, she wouldn't look at me. She didn't speak. Her arms folded over her chest. Not even my little dog, Mitzi, lying in the corner, was moving. When I reached out, calling "Itzi," she whimpered. My mother disappeared behind the curtained arched door, and I followed her to the kitchen where I stood, pulling on the hem of her cotton dress.

"Ma Ma." I raised my arms to her, but she wouldn't look down at me. "Ma Ma." Why was everyone ignoring me? *Why wouldn't my mother talk? Why wouldn't my big sister get up and play with me?*

Chapter 2

VANISHED

Deserts of West Texas: 1952

By the time I was four, I could not express how I felt about the breathtaking changes in my life. The disappearance of half my family, overnight, following the death of my sister to what I would later learn was acute lymphoblastic leukemia (ALL), the sudden departure of my father–who left and never returned–and my mother's withdrawal into a pool of grief. I couldn't fathom why, before I could catch my breath, my mother remarried a dark, troubled man and, quickly, we moved three hundred miles away from the town where I was born, deep into the desert.

Just like that, everyone was gone, disappeared. The tiny house we had lived in, a few blocks from my grandparents, gone. My puppy, gone. My life, also gone. I cried every day, until it brought on stomach aches that felt like rats chewing up my insides. When my mother scolded me, I'd run to my bedroom and lie face down on the hard floor, pressing my stomach into the wood, to distract myself from the pain. Or I'd go outside and lay across my swing, pushing my tummy into the seat. When I begged my mother to tell me why everyone disappeared, she said, "Forget it. That was ancient history. It's time to move on."

No one explained abandonment to me, and as a child I didn't know why my father left or why my mother married a man who uprooted us—my younger brother, my mother, and me—moving us away from the only home I had known. I didn't know that within a couple of years, I'd be moved to another continent and never allowed to see my father again. I didn't know that death meant I'd never see my sister again either. The one thing I did know was that the wind always blew up a storm when someone disappeared from my life. And I was pretty sure that, like the wind, my stepfather–a thin, nervous man, quick to anger, who drove too fast for children unbuckled in the back seat of his car–had a part in my suffering. So I listened for the sounds of an approaching windstorm and watched him for signs that he might bring more harm to one of us.

One evening after dinner, he pulled out a cigar and kicked his chair back, watching my mother clear dishes from the table. I hated the smell and usually threw up when he smoked in the house.

"Finish your dinner, kids!" He opened a can of beer and gave us more orders. "Chew with your mouth closed. Sit up in that chair!" I hated being ordered around even more than his smoking. Suddenly, he and my mother disappeared into the bathroom. "I'm going to help your mama take a bath," he said.

My little brother, Jon, and I got out of our chairs and went to the bathroom door, where we stood, a curious four-year-old and a trusting eighteen-month-old. We heard the thud of the rusty plunger closing and listened as water filled the old iron tub.

A few minutes later, we heard water draining and, suddenly, my mother screamed.

"Help!!!"

On the other side of the door, my stepfather's voice echoed. "Help." Then, "Oh no, she's gone down the drain!"

I no longer knew what wasn't possible when it came to disappearing, so I imagined that my mother had melted and vanished. I began to scream. My little brother jumped up and down, crying. Suddenly, the door yanked open, and they both emerged laughing. A dark shadow seemed to step across the doorsill toward me, and I moved back.

At night, when the house was dark, and the only sound was the West Texas wind whipping stars across the immense black sky, I'd lie awake, listening to the howling, wondering if a gale could blow through our house, pick me up, and take me deeper into the desert. I'd try to push my body deeper into the mattress for protection, and wondered, *where is the Jesus who 'loves me,' the one I sang to in Sunday School classes I attended at my grandmother's church back in my hometown? Did he know that we had been swept away, moved to a different town in West Texas? Did he know I was no longer in class? No longer in the little Methodist Church? Did anyone know I was gone? That I lived on the margins of the desert, where I was held prisoner in a land beneath a sun that ruled over everyone?*

I believed my only way to survive was to make my stepfather disappear. *After all, people could go away without warning. My sister and father had been swept away, hadn't they? I had been disappeared too.* I promised myself and secretly promised Jon, too, I'd do something to make him leave. I didn't know what it would take, but it would be something so bad that he'd want to be free of us.

One night as I lay in bed, the wind whispered ideas to me. Notions of revenge. The next morning, as the sun rose over the desert, the sky opened quietly. *No clouds. No wind. Not even a breeze. It was a perfect day for a crucifixion.* I remembered a large rusty nail I'd found under the front porch. It would make a good weapon.

I decided to attack my stepfather's prized possession, a '57 maroon Ford he called "Baby." I slithered under the porch and found the nail. Crawling backwards on my hands and knees, I reached daylight, stood up, back to the sun, raised my arm, and plunged the nail into the car's violet skin. Carefully, I slid the tip down the passenger door, and as I carved, the paint gave way, revealing a silvery metal. When trauma cuts lines so deep into the soul, a mark remains. I was proud of the attack; in my mind, it left evidence of my vanishing and gave voice to my despair. It was a symbolic act on my part–one that I would not fully understand for another fifty years–a first attempt at releasing pain into story.

Chapter 3

EXILED

The Deserts of West Texas (and Spain): 1949-1951

The legendary nine-hundred-mile-long Pecos River, which carries water across West Texas, has been depicted as a geographical division between civil society in the east and desolate lawlessness in the west. In the oft-misquoted John Wayne movie, Chisum, the protagonist proclaims, "There's no law west of Dodge and no God west of the Pecos River." This wild environment gave birth to the phrase "to pecos" someone, the practice of murdering a person and rolling his body into the river. The river flows down the Sangre de Cristo Mountains in north central New Mexico and crosses into West Texas, where it snakes across the Pecos River Valley, an area known by cowboys as the "real west." On the eastern side of the river, the climate is subtropical sub-humid, with hot summers and dry winters. On the western side is the driest part of the Longhorn State, with vast deserts broken up by rocky mountain peaks, sitting obediently under a boundless sky and an interminable sun. Survival demands a toughness of body and spirit, an ability to wrangle life in a way celebrated in stories about the stark, hostile environment.

13

I knew I was in trouble on the day my stepfather drove us across the Chihuahuan Desert to our new home, just outside the town of Salt Flat. My little brother and I craned our necks to see out the windows as we passed miles of glistening white sand, beneath the peaks of the Guadalupe Mountain Range. We stopped along the way on Highway 190, so my mother could read the historic plaque that marked the site of a large salt and mineral pan, the remnant of an ancient shallow lake from the Pleistocene Epoch, where, in the 19th century, hundreds of lives were lost in the San Elizario Salt War, fought over possession of the land and its minerals. Today, Salt Flat is little more than a couple of wooden house frames, an abandoned rock building, and miles of windblown sand. Tourists on the way to nearby Guadalupe State Park are often enticed by the sparkling sand and, unaware of danger, drive across the powdery stuff only to sink quickly. Sometimes they have to be rescued.

As soon as we crossed the cattle guard of the old iron gate that opened to the oil and gas camp, I felt sick to my stomach and begged to get out of the car. When my stepfather finally stopped, I opened the door to see miles of flat land littered with rusted bits of pipe and unrecognizable pieces of machines, skeletal remains of the oil and gas industry.

I ran to my mother and grabbed her arm. "Ma Ma, where are we?" It looked like we had left the earth and landed on an inhospitable planet, a world with a never-ending horizon. There were no trees or grass. Vertical metal pipes stood in rows, spewing out foul-smelling natural gas. Aside from the howling wind, nothing moved but oil pump jacks lifting the hammer and dropping it back down at a loud, rhythmic pace. Whoosh. Crack. We got back into the car and drove deeper into the camp, passing a large weathered, wooden building, which housed a kitchen and mess hall for workers.

A few hundred feet away, on a corner lot, our house stood on wooden stakes, most of its sage green paint peeled away by the sun and wind.

"Where are we?" I asked again and again. A question that would linger in my heart for years. On our first night in the house, the roof wailed a slow, sorrowful tune and the oil pump jacks drummed on, echoing across the hard land. I covered my head with a scratchy army blanket and cried myself to sleep.

I came to believe in the wind as a spirit, a dangerous one that wanted to pick me up and carry me away. One hot spring morning, I stretched across the back of the couch in the front room, looking out the big picture window for evidence of dust blowing across the yard. Suddenly, a gust plunged from atop the mountain peak, picking up sand and turning it into whirling tunnels, dancing across the desert floor. For hours, windstorms tore through the camp, filling the sky with pieces of earth, turning white clouds into reddish, misshapen monsters. Heavy pieces of old metal blew across the unpaved camp road and buildings heaved and squealed.

That afternoon, I hid out in the shade of the screen-covered back porch, prying loose splinters of wood from the floor, listening to Hank Williams on my mother's radio, as he sang about being so lonesome he could cry. Suddenly, the wind got wilder, and the radio announcer broke in to say something about a tornado in the area. That night, the storm blew clouds away from our part of the desert and thousands of twinkling lights appeared across the velvet sky. As I fell asleep, Hank Williams' lyrics echoed in my mind.

The next morning, I decided to look for help from someone in the camp. It was dangerous here and I wanted to escape, to go home. Before the noontime heat built up, I wandered over to the mess hall. Melba, the camp manager's wife with an Aunt Bee bun atop her head and a flowered apron covering her house dress, was in the kitchen cooking for the workers. I stood close, watching as she moved from the counter to the stove, dropping flour-coated chicken into hot oil popping in two huge cast iron skillets. The smell of chicken frying reminded me of the Sunday dinners I remembered my grandmother cooking. My grandmother, who I called Mommy, raised chickens in the backyard. When she was ready to make a meal, she'd grab a bird by the neck, twist until it snapped, cut off the head, and plunge the dead chicken into a huge cauldron of boiling water. Then she'd pluck the feathers, cut up the bird, and fry it in her big kitchen. The dinner she'd served looked nothing like the pets I'd seen wandering around the yard.

Grease popped and I backed out of Melba's path, peeking around the corner into the cavernous dining hall to get a glimpse of the cowboys who sat on backless benches around oilcloth-covered tables, hunched over plates of pinto beans. Hats and leather gloves were placed on the floor beneath the benches. Finally, I got the nerve to speak.

"Melba, do you know where I can find my daddy?"

She smiled and shushed me away, saying she was "too busy to talk right now."

"But he's a cowboy," I pleaded, thinking that would help. I wanted to ask her more: "Where is this place? Are we still in Texas? Where is the rest of my family?" I might have asked her, "Is this hell?" I wondered why no one — not even my grandparents — had come to rescue us. Thinking about all this brought back the pain in my stomach and I turned around and ran home.

The hot months grew into long, dark chilly days and weeks. When finally the sun began to warm the desert again, my mother went to the hospital. She was gone for four days, and Melba brought food to the house every night: green beans, cornbread, chicken fried steak. I was terrified my mother had left us or been taken away by a grisly beast or the wind. My stomach aches grew more intense, so in bed I'd curl up into a fetal position, listening for the sounds of imaginary wild animals running across the camp, ghoulish desert demons hovering over our house, waiting for a chance to come inside when everyone had fallen asleep.

On the day my mother came home, she walked in, a big smile on her face. "Hello, kids. I'm back."

I squealed. My mother was safe. She looked unscathed and she was smiling. *Why was she smiling when I had been so terrified?* I ran across the room toward her, but she stopped me, holding me back a bit. Behind her, my stepfather came through the door, carrying a tiny baby, wrapped in a delicate pink blanket. He sat on the sofa and motioned to Jon and me, "Come, peek at your new sister."

"Isn't she beautiful?" my mother said. Immediately, the baby began to scream. She didn't stop for years.

How could she have appeared without anyone telling me? People appeared and disappeared in my life without warning. That's when I knew we were never going home again. Like my sister and father, I had been disappeared and no one was coming to this desolate place to find me. I had been terrified for my mother's safety while she was gone and I wanted to elicit a promise from her, some sort of confirmation that she wouldn't go away again. But for the next few weeks, she was busy with the baby. As I watched her with my new sister, I realized I was no longer the baby sister, nor my father's youngest daughter. I was living in a land of lost children who were swept away by the wind, in a home where sorrow had come to stay.

For the next ten years of my life, I disappeared deeper. We moved every couple of years and each move took me farther away from home. At the same time, my family changed, adding more children. By the time I was eight years old, there were six of us — four children and two adults. Only three of us had survived the original family. My stepfather joined the Air Force, and we moved from West Texas to the state of Oklahoma, where we moved three times into new houses.

In another two years, we boarded an old Army ship in the New York Harbor that took us across the Atlantic Ocean and the North Sea to England. While there, we moved twice. Two years later, we moved to Spain, where we lived in a hotel for several months and then in an apartment for the next two years. We traveled over Europe, crossing geographic boundaries, learning new cultures, and taking in different landscapes. We took trips to Brussels, France, Switzerland to see the Alps, Germany, and

Italy to visit a castle where my stepfather had been stationed during World War II. Our moves were often made without much notice, and we were allowed to pack only what could be carried in our suitcases or moving boxes. I watched my mother constantly, worried that she'd be left behind. In the back of my mind, *I wondered, what if she disappears, too?*

Chapter 4

ESCAPED

Europe: 1959

Military orders kept my family in Europe for nearly four years, making it impossible for me to be found by my father. Besides, my mother claimed he abandoned us before she uprooted me and moved me away. I was confused by his departure. No one called this abandonment in the mid-1950s and there were no international laws protecting children from much of anything. I suppose I still believed it possible that someone would come to rescue me. Or, magically, that someone distantly related to my Texas family would find me in Europe. I was a lonely, bewildered, and homesick child.

The desperate need to find my way home was always with me and it hit particularly hard one hot afternoon in Spain. My family had moved to the city of Zaragoza, just outside one of the new military bases built during the reign of the dictator Francisco Franco. We lived in a very large fifth-story apartment. On that scorching day, my parents decided to head to the base commissary to shop for groceries and to drag four children along with them. For some reason, they thought it would be a good idea to take the base shuttle bus rather than drive the car twenty miles to the base.

We left our apartment in the heat of the day–during siesta–walking across the central part of the city. We walked down the tree-lined promenade and across the roundabout to the busiest street in Zaragoza, to stand beneath the fountain where we waited for the bus. We dipped our hands into the cool water, watching as small black cars and motorcycles whizzed by at such high speeds that if one of us had stepped off the sidewalk, we'd surely have been hit. After waiting for what seemed like an eternity, the old bus arrived, and we rushed up the steps and toward the back of the bus. Open windows allowed some of the steaming wind to blow through the bus, but it didn't help much. My parents and three siblings sat in the back row, but there wasn't room for me. My stepfather waved me toward an empty seat in front of him. A young Spanish teenager sat by the window, so I motioned to him and took the seat on the aisle. I was shy about sitting so close to him and began to scout around the bus for another empty seat, spotting one just two rows ahead of me.

When I stood up to move, my stepfather yelled, "Where are you going? Sit down, now!"

My face burned with embarrassment. I had to think of something to explain my move, so I responded, "I see something on the floor. I think it's money." Sure enough, a peso was on the ground under the seat in front of me, so I quickly bent over and picked it up. "Here it is," I said.

"Just sit down," my stepfather yelled again. I wanted to

hide — he was so loud. It seemed that anytime we were in public, he behaved like a clown, a noisy, ugly American.

I sat back down and waited for the bus to move. The driver shoved the engine into gear, and we jumped back into heavy traffic, as he navigated his way across the busiest part of the city, darting in and out of lanes, ignoring small cars, honking at trucks and other buses. As we reached the edge of the city, I spotted the striking Roman Catholic Church that sat on the edge of the Ebro River. Two months earlier, at the end of my fifth-grade year, my teacher had taken us on a field trip to see the grand Basílica de Nuestra Señora del Pilar, known as El Pilar. For a week before the trip, we studied the history of the church, learning that it had been built and rebuilt by conquering nations to honor the Virgin Mary. Ancient tradition holds that while she was still living in Jerusalem, the Virgin Mary, accompanied by thousands of angels, appeared on the banks of the Ebro sometime around 40 A.D. to offer comfort to the Apostle Saint James. Mary asked James to build a church on the site and she left behind a pillar of jasper to mark her appearance.

The building was huge and its eleven brightly colored tile domes reflected the sun during the day. At night, the four giant towers and smaller patina-covered cupolas lit up the city's sky. I remembered standing inside the enormous church, waiting in the vestibule with my classmates, teacher, and my mother, who came along as a chaperone. The nun leading the tour motioned us to stand aside to allow room for small children to move down the center of the aisle. In broken English, she explained, they were waiting to participate in the ritual known as "The

Passing of Children," a tradition in which children walk close to the feet of the image of the Virgin Mary, stopping to pray for "shelter for them under her protective cloak." My mother, who was suspicious of the Catholic Church, did not like the practice and she said so. But I was deeply moved by the idea that a supernatural being could care enough to want to provide shelter for a child. This might have been the first time I was aware of a female sacred being concerned with the safety of children. On a deep level, it brought back memories of my sister, although I didn't know why at the time.

I was startled out of my reverie when the bus hit a bump, and one of the passengers in front dropped a small suitcase on the floor. The driver sped up as we entered the flat highway, flying across the road until we reached a tiny village a few kilometers away. He stopped at the square and several passengers rose and began to walk down the aisle to exit the bus.

An idea suddenly came to me. I would wait until the last person was ready to get off the bus; then I'd jump up and run to the front, hop down the steps and run around the back to cross the street. I could escape before anyone knew I was gone. This might be my chance to get away, to find Texas, and to finally find my father. I sat on the edge of the seat, waiting for the bus to empty, and as I watched people walk down the aisle, reality hit me. *I was living in a foreign country. I had no idea where Texas was, nor how to get back there.* I sat back down and stayed very still as the driver closed the door and the bus began to move again.

This was it, I thought. *I was living in a land where no one could find me. I'd never get home again.* I knew there was as much chance of my returning home to West Texas to my father as there was that the wind would stop blowing across the vast ocean that separated us. The reality was, no one in my family was going to help me find my father and no one cared how much pain this caused me. I was no more important than an extra passenger on the bus. The boy sitting beside me lowered the window and the hot wind gushed through the small opening, stinging my face, a reminder that I was not able to do anything about being disappeared.

By the time we returned to the United States, I had fallen into a pattern of life defined by disappearance, disruption, and fear. My desire to go home to Texas to find my father and learn the real story behind his departure clashed with a fear of upsetting my mother, creating a tension that I carried into adolescence, through my teen years, and, in many ways, into my adulthood. I felt unsafe in the world and longed for a haven where I could exist without fear of abandonment or loss. Eventually, I found such a place by turning inward, where I lived in my imagination. The place Robert Louis Stevenson described in *Across The Plains* as the "phantasmagoric chamber" of my brain, "with the painted windows and the storied wall." Inside these walls, I was protected from the ever-shifting landscape of the outer world. In my imagination, I was in control. No one vanished. And, if they did, I could create them again in the form of a new person. After years of upheaval and sudden moves, I exiled myself to an imaginary sphere. Story became a place for me to go, a destination where I would never have to worry about unbearable loss or upheaval. Story would keep me safe. Or so I believed.

Chapter 5

LEFT BEHIND

San Angelo, Texas: 1969

Sixteen years after the big vanishing, I stood at the back of the little wood chapel on the military base in San Angelo, Texas. I was dressed in a white lace suit, my dark hair pulled into a tight French twist with tiny white bows scattered across the back of my head. Outside, the November wind whistled, blowing dried tumbleweed across the desert floor. Just as the organist began to play the wedding march, I looked down the aisle where my fiancé stood and tried to breathe.

I turned to my stepfather, whispering, "I can't do this. I might disappear."

He laughed, then, in his military officer voice, ordered me, "Walk down that aisle and don't look back."

I wasn't aware of walking, but when I looked down at my feet, the dark red carpet seemed to pull me forward as though it would open up and swallow me. I reached the altar, and my soon-to-be-husband took my hand and guided me to my place next to him. It felt more like a surreal ritual than a wedding.

All I could think was, *my life of abandonment-by-disappearance was about to unfold again in a new chapter – the same painful plot was going to repeat.* I was not yet twenty and had no idea how to exit in the middle of a ceremony, with a chapel full of people.

I turned to look at my stepfather, remembering the warning he had given me a few years earlier. "You are not the kind of young woman any man would want to marry," he had said. At the time I didn't understand, but that morning, something made me wonder if he was right. *Was there something about me that drove men away?* Still, deep in my soul, I felt something I couldn't ignore–the presence of the elements for disaster: wind, desert, a man with dark features. I froze, standing like a statue, an ice queen, as people watched me recite wedding vows.

"I do," he said.

"I do," I whispered. Even as the words came out of my mouth, I knew I was falling across a threshold that would lead me into a new era of life, initiated into a role I wasn't sure I could follow. After the ceremony, we left the chapel for a tiny reception at the nearby officer's club, where guests filled the room. Gifts and cards were at one end of the white linen-covered table, candelabras and white and pink gladiolus flowers in the center. Champagne was served with heavily-frosted cake and petit-fours, chicken salad, and cucumber sandwiches. So much white, it was dizzying.

"Congratulations." My younger sister's voice was weak as she spoke. My mother, with her silvery hair, looked beautiful in her aqua silky shift and white gloves, but she could not stop frowning. We posed for a few photographs and an hour later, I threw my bouquet of white carnations and delicate pink roses over my shoulder. It landed on the floor. A foreshadowing of the years to come.

We departed for an overnight honeymoon in a nearby hotel by the river in the city. The following week, we moved our meager furnishings–a queen size brass headboard and mattress and a long piece of lumber we put atop cinder blocks for a dining table–into our studio apartment in downtown San Angelo, above the blood bank. Even today, decades later, when I look through old photos of the wedding, I see the dazed look on the face of a young bride who is watching a disastrous accident about to happen. She seems to understand on some level that she has placed herself in the path of a story over which she has no control.

Carlisle, Pennsylvania: 1976

Twenty-five hundred miles across the country, seven years later, we moved into our new home in southeastern Pennsylvania. The winter wind howled outside, freezing the marigolds that remained in the beds beneath the front windows, the ones I just couldn't find the energy to pull out before the frost arrived. I stood in the living room, where Fisher Price toys were scattered across the shag rug. Over the sound of the Grateful Dead playing in the background and our Scottish terrier Magoo barking, I said to my husband, "I want a divorce."

Even though my first misgivings about marriage had dissolved into joy for the first five years we were together, if I'm being honest, they were also filled with humiliation and pain, all brought on by my husband's infidelity. A year earlier, when we moved into the new two-story colonial house, guarded by white pillars, I'd tried to decorate the magic back into the relationship. To revive the love that had disappeared. Green appliances in the kitchen, sunny yellow for my oldest son's room. Robin's egg blue for the baby's crib. Flowered pillows on the bed. None of it, I discovered, was charming enough to keep me in a marriage with a man whose behavior–drinking and multiple affairs–was intolerable. Abandonment was still abandonment, even when dressed up in chintz fabric.

"I can't live without you. I'd rather be dead. I really will end my life if you leave me," he said, lighting a cigarette. He knew I'd object to his smoking in the house. *Was he trying to distract me by engaging me in an argument or is this his way of punctuating his threat? Making his threat more threatening?* I didn't care. I reminded myself of all I'd survived. I could do this.

"OK. Do what you want, but this marriage is over." We had been in couples counseling for months, but it had made no difference. He was still the handsome poetry-writing charmer who wanted to be married one day and single on other days. His affairs with women who were my acquaintances had worn me down. Not even I, who had been taught to live with abandonment, could accept prolonged infidelity. The ultimate form of disappearance.

"I will lose my mind if I stay married to you. So one of us has to go," I told him. A few weeks later, he left the house, moving in with a co-worker, a woman he'd known for less than a year. For months afterwards, I cried myself to sleep. One chilly evening, about six weeks into the separation, I must have been weeping loudly.

My four-year-old son walked into my bedroom. "It's alright, Mommy. It's alright," he said.

I hugged him and told him, "Mommy just had a bad dream. Let's go back to sleep now." He climbed in next to me, snuggled under my arm, and was asleep quickly. I was lost and lonely, living across the country from my family. No one understood my decision to end my marriage. My husband's family–whom I had protected from knowing about his affairs–was angry at me. My friends thought I should forgive my husband and stay in the marriage; the counselor chose a neutral position but showed very little compassion. *Why wouldn't anyone support me?* I wondered. Our marriage was broken, in the way poets had described the world after the First World War, considered one of the deadliest global conflicts in history. It was "broken in two." Not even my friends' rejection of my decision could discourage me. In fact, I felt a sense of power, even a little bit of victory for extricating myself from a painful union. I told myself I was searching for a bigger story. I wanted to lean into the future, to feel something more than mere survival, and it would not happen with this man.

Months later, on the day I signed sales papers and loaded my belongings into a U-Haul truck, I looked over my shoulder and said, "I'm finished with this confusing life story." I picked up suitcases and loaded them into the trunk of the little red economy car I bought with the money I'd made selling the house and coaxed my two little boys, ages two and four, into the back seat.

Just that fast, I left, pulled by a pattern established early in my childhood, defined by a complex mixture of losing, leaving, deserting, yearning to be found. Withdrawing from the external world into my own solitude had become a form of comfort for me. Now I was free to sink deep into my imagination where I could create a new life, one of stability and safety. As I drove away, the colonial house of my former dreams began to recede in the rear-view mirror, leaving only a fog of memory. What I could not have seen and could not have known was that, buried deep in the suitcases in the trunk, was the soul of a tiny child carrying an untold family fable. A story that would not disappear.

Chapter 6

DIMINISHED

Carlisle, Pennsylvania: 1977

It had been my choice to leave my marriage. I had been the one to end the relationship. I would no longer be the object of the verb to disappear, no longer the woman who accepted the dismissive action of a stronger voice in the sentence. But along with my freedom came the reopening of the hollow place where my childhood losses lived inside me. Painful stomach aches filled the emptiness in my body. Sleep was elusive and filled with vivid nightmares when I was able to close my eyes for more than an hour. The adult woman who chose to end an unbearable relationship had inadvertently reopened the wound carved into the soul of the little child and the needs of both came crashing down on me. *How could it be, I wondered, that doing what seemed right would cause me more suffering?*

On some level, I understood the source of the pain was more than my divorce, the loss of the man I had to admit I still loved. Part of the ache came from the dance of anger I was locked in with my mother, the person I thought responsible for teaching me how it felt to be lost, forgotten.

One evening, several months after the separation, I stood at the kitchen sink washing dishes, as the sun set outside my window. I had moved my boys and myself into a duplex on the north side of town where the rent was affordable. I put down the pot I was scrubbing and looked out the window at the giant full moon clearing the horizon, and felt it pulling sorrow and fear up from someplace deep inside me. Tears filled my eyes. I couldn't pay my rent for the month. The only thing in the refrigerator was an open can of cat food. *How would I make it through the night, let alone the month?* I had spent months working low-paying entry level jobs and the reality of supporting two children without financial or emotional help settled in. I was alone, broke, and angry.

Just that morning, I had rolled down my window and yelled at the crossing guard on the corner stopping traffic to allow school children to walk across the street. Earlier in the week, I screamed at the television and snarled at my son's pre-school teacher. I argued on the phone with my ex-husband for failing to make court-ordered child support payments. A week earlier, I had stood in the courtroom, asking the judge to impose a fine on him, to force him to pay.

"I cannot survive without these payments," I said, shoving a file filled with bills and receipts onto his bench. The checks were so small, they must have seemed insignificant to the judge. But, for me, they meant survival.

He responded with a ridiculous statement. "If I fine him, he'll have less money to pay you."

I looked around the room, searching for a compassionate set

of eyes, someone who would affirm my feelings of helplessness. But no one moved, no one smiled, not one person looked at me. *Did they not hear what this judge said to me?*

"You are supposed to be helping me, not making excuses for a deadbeat!" I raised my voice at him, and his eyebrows arched over his glasses.

He pulled himself up in his chair and smiled at me as he spoke. "You know the old saying, ma'am. You can't bleed a stone."

Furious, I grabbed my bag and my bills and whirled around, stomping out of the courtroom. *Just let him charge me with contempt of court. How could I fight a system that clearly was set up to maintain the status quo?*

Two months earlier, the same judge had declined to enforce child support payments because I refused to let my sons visit their father. I had good reason. They had come home from the last two visits in tears, saying, "Daddy locked himself in the bedroom all weekend, Mommy. He told us he'd love us more if you loved him." I was heartbroken to hear this from my two little boys. Immediately, I contacted the judge and told him of my plans.

It all came down on me as I stood in the kitchen. *What am I supposed to do? I cannot get what I need to feed my own children without endangering them.* I was angry that, as a woman, I had never been paid at the same level as the men who worked jobs similar or equal to mine. I had no support system from either side of my family. No one offered help with childcare. My landlord was sending me threatening eviction notices. I couldn't afford to put gas in the car. No one came forward to help in any way. Rage didn't touch the depth of my feelings about the situation.

So, yes, I became a loud, angry divorced woman. Maybe I believed raising the volume of my voice would disguise the terror I carried. *Perhaps*, I thought, *speaking up would discourage anyone else from trying to take advantage of me.* Alone and frightened, I had to do something to take care of us. Weeks later, when I came across an ad in the weekly paper for an entry-level job as an announcer at the local radio station, I jumped on it. *Why not use my voice to earn a paycheck?* I thought.

Five days later, wearing my navy-blue blazer, I stepped into the recording studio of the station. I sat down before the microphone and read a couple of wire stories. The station owner and program director stood behind me, listening. "Today, the Prime Minister of Israel, Yitzhak Shamir, was…." I read.

The owner stopped me, mid-sentence, and said, "Come to work early Monday." The salary he offered wasn't great, but it was a beginning.

My first morning on the job, I arrived at five a.m., climbed the stairs to the broadcast studio on the second floor, and walked into the tiny newsroom. The floor and walls were covered in carpet to enhance the acoustics. A police scanner squawked and a weather radio blasted forecasts for all the counties in southeastern Pennsylvania. An Associated Press newswire sat in the corner, next to a long desk with microphones. But there was no heat, so I kept my coat on as I scanned the local newspaper, ripped off a section of news from the wire machine, and wrote up a three-minute newscast. Of course, I had to guess the length since I'd never done this before. I had been given a tour of the station three days ago and "told" what to do, but I was not provided any training.

Terrified, I sat down in front of the microphone, adjusting it to meet my face. My hands shook as I watched the oversized clock on the wall above me, waiting for the second hand to hit fifty-nine minutes after the hour when ABC Network News ended. *Four more minutes. Can I really do this?*

Someone pounded on the wooden door of the newsroom, and the program director, a thirty-something from the coal region of the state, walked in. He pulled a handkerchief out of his back pocket, blew his nose, and informed me, "I just want you to know we only hired you because you help us meet minority requirements required by the FCC." He laughed as though someone had told a joke. *OK, so this is how it's going to be,* I thought. Van Gorge—his radio name—turned and walked back down the hall, entered the control room, sat down, and opened my microphone.

"This," he announced in a what was known in the broadcast field as the delivery style of a yukker, "is Jane Hollinger, our new morning anchor." His voice oozed with AM radio talk-show bluster. I didn't know whether to panic and run out the front door, or to scream back at him. *Too late. I was on the air.* I dug down deep inside and pulled up a determination I didn't know existed in me.

"Good morning, it's 6:04 on this chilly February morning. Here are the day's headlines." My indignation over Gorge's remark disguised the fear in my voice. When I finished the short newscast, he closed the mic and I jumped up, ripping off the headphones. *I did it. I can do it!*

It was the beginning of a fifteen-year career in which I

became known across Pennsylvania as one of few female voices recognized by a large audience. Within six months, without realizing it, I had become a so-called celebrity. People recognized my name in town. Listeners called me at the radio station and other newscasters in the area sought me out for ledes on stories. The other men on staff, all of them wannabe Howard Sterns, were just as offensive and sexist as Van, but I didn't care. I was on my way. Looking back, I know the little four-year old girl who dragged a nail across her stepfather's car was with me in the newsroom every day. She was the energy behind my voice.

The media industry thrived on dissent, so I was in the right arena to cultivate a fierceness that would propel me through some difficult years. A day job where I could take on the persona of a tough, professional newswoman was the perfect outlet for the frightened little girl and for the woman worried about feeding her children.

The next few years were a mixture of stress and excitement as my career and reputation grew. There was never enough money. I juggled bills every month, paying the water bill one time and skipping the electric bill. Buying day-old bread and meat that was on sale, just to have enough to purchase school clothes. The stress kept me up at night, all night. At one point, I moved back to Texas to accept a job as morning anchor with a powerful FM radio station offering me a higher salary. But my sons missed their family in Pennsylvania. I had to choose between losing sleep over money and the stress caused by keeping my sons so far away from their father. Feeling that they needed stability, I returned to Carlisle, to the low-paying position I had left six months earlier. The work was grueling. During the week, my days at the station began at four in the morning, and it was not unusual for me to show up without any sleep and work a ten-to-twelve-hour day.

One morning, as I sat in the newsroom looking over my script for the day's final newscast, the station receptionist buzzed me. "I have a call waiting for you. A man who says he's from the Associated Press."

Wondering what to expect, I answered the phone when it rang. Chris, a manager with the news outlet, spoke. "Hello, Jane. I'm calling because we need a journalist to anchor legislative news for the broadcast division in Harrisburg. Your name has come up as a candidate. Can you have lunch with me tomorrow?"

The next day after my shift, I met him at a local pub, and we talked about the position. Before we left, I signed a contract with the AP and within a month, I had given notice at the radio station and moved into the newsroom at the State Capitol building in Harrisburg. I was thrilled to leave behind the rinky-dink local station and the likes of Van Gorge.

To say my job was exciting is an understatement. Months of running across the state chasing down news, often involving the misuse of taxpayers' money or abuse of power. At the time, the Pennsylvania Legislature was known for questionable, sometimes crooked back-door deals, brokered by legislative leaders looking to fill their pockets while building power. I was never at a loss for interesting news stories. My reports were broadcast several times a day on 45 to 50 radio stations across the state, and I developed a following, a fairly sizeable group of listeners who became fans of my Capitol reports. It was exhilarating to work in an industry where my voice was respected and where I was making broadcast history for women. But my success came at a price. It was the 1980s, a time when women were seen as embellishments on the news set, judged for the flip of our locks and size of our waists. Sexual harassment was so prevalent that no one bothered to hide it.

One October evening, a few months after moving to the Capitol, I traveled to Pittsburgh with my boss to attend a conference for journalists. On the first evening, we gathered at the posh Omni William Penn Hotel in Pittsburgh, with a large group of journalists for dinner. Afterward, we walked into a smaller conference room for an evening party. The room was stunning: large-coffered ceilings, gold-embossed wallpapered walls, arched entries. I stood in a small circle of my colleagues, near a baby grand piano, sipping cocktails.

I was aware of being the only woman in my group, which included my immediate boss and his boss, the regional director of the international wire service I worked for. I became somewhat nervous. Although my feet were aching from wearing heels during the day's long meetings and planning sessions, I decided to be polite and stay for a while. Besides, I wanted to belong. As they drank, the conversation became lively. One man loosened the top button of his shirt. The laughter grew boisterous, and I thought it was time to find a way to make an exit before things got unmanageable.

Broadcast journalists were not known for political correctness, nor for avoiding sexist, racist jokes and comments. I finished my drink and set the empty glass on the mahogany table and, just as I began to walk away, the big boss Gerald, standing across from me, smiled. His broad, overly tanned face seemed to smirk as he said, "Jane, how about if you come to my room for another drink. We can have several drinks."

"Wh…what?" I said. Gerald had been promoted recently, having made his mark as an ace reporter, a tough inner city Philadelphia journalist. Privately, my colleagues questioned his ability to manage. A tone of entitlement dripped off his tongue as he repeated what I knew was a request.

Before he finished, I cut him off. "I've got to get to my room and call my sons before bedtime." Having two teenagers at home four hours away gave me an excuse to leave without having to openly confront Gerald.

I looked around for support from the other men, but no one spoke, not even my immediate boss, a highly principled, white-haired Catholic. The Oxford shirts didn't move. No one seemed to think this was an unusual situation. Solicitous comments were not considered to be inappropriate — at least, not in this industry. I felt alone. And I was furious. Gerald was my boss's boss. He had just made a suggestive demand of me in front of everyone! I didn't excuse myself; rather I turned around and walked across the big room and out of the door. *Jerks! All of them!*

The next day, my boss Ray and I rushed to catch the Amtrak train to travel back to the office in the Capitol Building in Harrisburg. I sat next to him and for a while, we discussed newsroom business, political coverage, and the upcoming elections. As the train entered the Allegheny National Forest of western Pennsylvania, we watched the view outside the windows, acres of trees displaying translucent fall-colored leaves. The train began to gain altitude, and we reached the curved stretch of tracks, known as the Horseshoe Bend near Altoona, considered an engineering wonder that allows trains to make a gradual climb up the mountains and down on the other side. Maybe it was the dramatic descent into the valley— I'd always responded to the beauty of mountains and forests. But I couldn't hold onto my feelings about the previous night's events any longer. I had felt alone, just like the tiny child at her sister's funeral, when no one would speak to her or comfort her.

I turned to face Ray and asked him if he had felt uncomfortable with Gerald's comments. He was silent, but I knew he saw my anger. I pressed him.

"Did you not see this as a form of harassment? How could you stand there and not speak up when he invited me to his room?!"

His usually pale Irish face turned red, nearly purple. "I thought he was just being friendly."

"Friendly! Ray, he was posturing, showing everyone he could use his position to ask the single woman to come to his hotel room. It was a display of power. He was trying to impress everyone at my expense. He owes me an apology." *And so do you,* I wanted to say.

I was angry at having to explain what I knew was obvious. I got up and moved across the aisle. The train continued to move east, lulling me into a more relaxed state. It occurred to me that I had been speaking for the child in me who felt so lost, the little girl who didn't have the language to ask questions about the sudden disappearances of her sister and father. Still, I didn't talk to Ray for the rest of the ride.

Several days later as we sat in the office, Ray got up and walked into the small room where six news wire machines were pounding out the day's events from around the world.

"Can we talk?" he asked. I joined him, trying to hear his apology over the sound of the machines. "I'm sorry I didn't speak up for you." I knew he didn't want anyone else in the office to hear his apology.

I thanked him and nothing more came of the situation. In spite of my show of bravado in speaking up, I spent weeks worrying about the fallout that could come from scolding my boss. I could not afford to lose my job.

Within three years, I landed a position as the news director of a statewide broadcast news organization, where I supervised an all-male news team. I arrived with a tougher skin and an intolerance for misogyny. My new position at the network required me to hire, train, and supervise about a dozen men. I came to the network with positive expectations about the position, but it didn't take long to learn how the men felt about having a woman as a boss. Over the months, I experienced the costs imposed on women who held positions of power, in the form of lost friendships and snide, snarky remarks made behind my back.

One morning I walked into the large newsroom where we gathered, wrote, edited, and reported news, sports, and weather. It was a crowded, noisy room. Six men, including Jack, a bombastic-voiced sports reporter, were gathered in a circle, complaining that I was being paid $10,000 a year more than them. "That's not fair," Jack said.

I thought, *It was unfair. As the boss. Who worked twelve-hour days. Who had written the entire program, consisting of twelve hours of news, sports, and weather. Imagine that. I deserved more. More money, more respect.*

Jack's face fell when he saw me. The others scuttled back to their desks and nothing more was said.

A few weeks later, I overhead laughter from my office. When I entered the newsroom, four of the guys were talking about giving me the name, "Cruella de Vil," after the villain in the movie *101 Dalmatians.* They broke into laughter until they saw me. Almost immediately, they fell silent. Hurt and angry, I grew more determined. For a few years, I was reluctant to date anyone in the news industry, knowing that some of the men wanted my job and would do almost anything–including lie about me–to get it. I felt especially vulnerable as a single mother of sons, fearful for my reputation.

One chilly February morning, the manager of the network, Donald, a large, rather garish man whose claim to fame was that he was the nephew of Milton Berle, called me into his office for a meeting. Matthew, the assistant manager, whose experience included a sales position for a local FM country radio station, joined us. Matthew was known for speaking to everyone in a pious, judgmental tone that revealed his sense of privilege. Years later, he would leave the broadcast industry to become a minister. The plush shag carpet and glowing fire in the ornate office lulled me into thinking I might be praised for my efforts as a female news director, who was responsible for producing news coverage for the network. I sank down in the Queen Anne chair, across the desk from "Uncle Militie's boy" and waited for a pat on the head. At least a "job well done." But what I got was very different.

The big boss took a sip of coffee, scrunched up his puffy face, and without even a morning greeting, said to me, "The men in the newsroom are afraid of you."

His remark stung. *How could he say this to me?* I wondered. *I was one of the only women in the country to be in this position. I was paving the way for women in the industry.* Still, my response was more defensive than I meant it to be.

"Good. I want them to be scared — otherwise, they will take advantage of me," I said. A few minutes later when the meeting ended, I left, feeling chagrined. For a minute, I was angry at myself for allowing the small, terrified child's voice to erupt into that of an adult woman. Then I wondered if Donald would have said such a thing to a male news director. I wondered how any woman would respond to being judged in this way. And to be honest, these men needed supervision. *After all,* I thought, *men in the broadcast industry tend to be prima donnas.*

I wanted to become an example for women who were willing to risk personal comfort by speaking up. I was trying to advance the rights of women in this profession. *Why,* I wondered, *did I run into so much resistance and push-back? More importantly, why did these reactions to my work trigger negativity, leading me to struggle with old feelings of shame, the same feelings invoked by my mother when I followed her around the house, trying to protect her?*

Chapter 7

BANISHED

Harrisburg, Pennsylvania: 1986

Over the years, I remained dedicated to advocacy journalism. I was driven by a desire to put myself in the path of powerful stories, often about the exploitation of others and injuries caused by those in power, as well as to speak up for those who were ignored by the system. Advocacy journalism gave me a way to redirect my angst, by using my voice to call for justice for the vulnerable. It was no longer just about my loss; I learned that all of humankind is coming to terms with harm every day. My voice became an instrument for expressing both my sorrow and that of others. But one experience made it clear that being an activist would come at a cost: as I spoke up for others, I had to learn to defend myself.

In the late 1980s during the abortion debates in the state legislature, spurred by the lawsuit filed against Planned Parenthood by Pennsylvania Governor Bob Casey, I became embroiled in a contentious and very public fight with a lawmaker who wanted to penalize women for using Medicaid to cover the cost of abortions. State Representative Stephen Freind was a former district attorney, a wiry, short, red-faced Republican congressman from Philadelphia. Freind authored the Abortion Control Act of 1982, which required, among other provisions, that a "married woman notify her husband" of her plans to terminate a pregnancy, and that doctors show patients a pamphlet with pictures of developing fetuses, as well as several other restrictions. All but the spousal notification requirements were upheld by the Supreme Court.

In 1988, Freind went after poor women again, proposing legislation that would severely punish welfare recipients for using federal money to cover the cost of abortions, even including a suggestion for jail time as a penalty. It was late in the afternoon when the debate over this bill erupted in the House of Representatives. I was sitting at my desk in the Capitol newsroom, editing reports, while listening to the session broadcast on speakers wired in the room. Several other reporters–almost all men–listened in but didn't seem to be particularly interested in the points Freind was making to his colleagues. My attention was piqued when he was challenged by a Democratic lawmaker who asked about providing exceptions in the bill for victims of rape. Freind responded, "Women who get raped don't get pregnant." I stopped what I was doing and walked over to the speaker.

Did he say what I thought I heard him say? "Victims of rape don't get pregnant."

I listened more closely as one or two lawmakers challenged him. He held his ground, repeating that it was "almost impossible" for a woman to become pregnant through rape. His reason for his outrageous claim? A report published weeks later in the Allentown Morning Call captured his explanation. Freind said the stress from sexual assault "causes her to secrete a certain secretion, which has a tendency to kill sperm."

I couldn't believe what I was hearing. His remarks touched a deep feeling in me, a place where I carried a profound sensitivity to being an underpaid, largely ignored woman. I was not much different from the women he wanted to target; I was a single parent, trying to take care of a family, struggling to make ends meet, living paycheck to paycheck. His political statement suddenly had become personal. Back on the floor of the House the debate flashed into a tirade, as Freind insisted he had proof to back up his claim about rape and pregnancy.

"Is he crazy? He can't mean this. He can't believe it."

I began to shake with anger. I grabbed my microphone, called the cameraman, and ran out of the room. I raced down the marble steps, across the Rotunda and into the House of Representatives, hoping to get a statement from Freind before he disappeared into his office. When I got to the door of the House Chamber, I stood in the rear, listening for the speaker's gavel. Bang! I ran down the blood-red carpet, past rows of ornate desks, past lawmakers dressed in expensive suits, to reach Freind's seat. He was talking with a staff member, so I waited.

Glancing up at the ceiling, my eyes focused on an ornate work of art painted with heavy oils, splashed with gold leaf. I had not noticed this in the past. Called *The Hours,* it represents the passage of time illustrated by 24 maidens circling, endlessly, around the moon, sun, and the stars of the Milky Way. Here I was, standing in the hallowed hall of the massive chamber built for the 130 members of the legislative body of state government, initiated by William Penn himself. A hall dominated, for the most part, by white men. *Was I merely dancing in a circle by chasing this news story? By trying to expose such a cruel attempt to punish women?*

Freind finished the conversation and turned to me, smiling. "Hi, Jane." He knew exactly what had brought me into the chamber, and I sensed his excitement about discussing his controversial legislation with a member of the media.

"Will you explain your theory of rape and pregnancy?" I asked.

"Sure, I'd be happy to do so," he smiled again as he spoke.

Where is the videographer? I wondered. I was afraid to wait any longer out of concern that reason would return to Freind, and I'd miss the story. So I decided to do the interview using my microphone and hand-held tape recorder. But he wasn't going to change his mind. He puffed up his chest, stepped forward, and began by explaining the bill, including the penalty he proposed for welfare recipients who used tax money to cover the cost of abortions.

"Why," I asked him, "would you want to punish poor women, the most vulnerable group in the state." It wasn't a question.

"These people are costing taxpayers too much," he said.

You, I thought, are costing taxpayers as well, with your overinflated salary and expense account.

Then, to add more punch, he said, "They should not be rewarded for using abortion as a form of birth control."

"Abortion as birth control?" *What is he talking about?* I pressed him to say more. I was getting anxious, wanting to push him to repeat his claim that rape victims never get pregnant. It didn't take much. "Please, Representative, explain your theory of rape and pregnancy."

"Oh, it's not my theory," he responded. He pulled a paper from his briefcase, waved it in the air and said, "Here's a medical report that supports my statement." Then, he repeated, "Women who get raped very seldom get pregnant. That's because when a traumatic experience is undergone, a woman secretes a certain secretion which has a tendency to kill sperm." His face contorted into that of a mad scientist (my apologies to scientists) as he spoke. He was pleased with himself.

"Can I have a copy of this report to use in my story?" I had to see this outlandish claim in writing. But he declined, quickly pulling it away and stuffing it inside his briefcase. *This man is either delusional or he's lying.*

"Will you tell me the name of the doctor who made this assertion? I'd like to speak with him."

"I will release everything when I'm ready to put forth the proposed legislation," he said.

When I'm ready, I thought. The arrogance!

"Thank you, Mr. Freind," I said, wrapping up the interview. I wasn't interested in arguing with him, nor in trying to get him to re-think his position. God knows he had plenty of staff to help him research the issue before crafting this piece of legislation. He had said exactly what he believed–that women on welfare had no rights. I turned and ran upstairs to the studio to produce the segment, which ran on the overnight wire and on the statewide radio network. My boss jumped on the report and ran it for several hours.

"What a wild story," he told me. "Try to do a follow-up piece for the morning news."

The report ran on multiple radio stations across the state for two or three days. Interestingly, only one or two of my male colleagues in the newsroom picked it up. Not only did most of them ignore the story, some weren't very happy about my decision to report it. Late on Friday afternoon, one of them approached me and shared his disdain.

"Jane, why are you doing this? You're ruining his career." This, from a reporter with the Philadelphia Inquirer Capitol bureau, a cigar puffing, sharp-tongued reporter. Rob considered himself to be a ringleader in the newsroom, but to me, he was a privileged white male who bragged about his Mercedes-Benz.

What could he know about being a poor woman? I, who was supporting children on a single salary, understood all too well. I felt the danger of this bill in my gut as a threat to all women. It was an attempt to control and silence us. I would not be quiet.

"No," I argued, *"he's* ruining it and I'm trying to stop him from ruining the lives of poor women who have been assaulted." I must have yelled, gauging from the looks on the faces of the other men in the room, who stopped their work, got up from their desks, and began to listen to us. "I have an obligation as a reporter to question such overreaches of power, blatant attempts to target poor women, and bring the information to the public."

Still, for days, the men balked. When I walked into the main newsroom to pick up my mail, smirks and smiles broke out on their faces. I knew they thought of me as a feminist, which was a somewhat negative or extreme concept in the late

1980s. Gradually, one or two newspapers picked up the story and eventually, it got more play. The major television networks covered it. Even the famous newspaper columnist Ann Landers wrote a piece about Freind's sexist claims. When the story got more exposure, Freind came under attack by educators and providers of rape counseling services in the area. Within a week the Kaiser Permanente Health Care Program in Reston, Virginia issued a statement on behalf of Dr. Fred Mecklenburg, an obstetrician/gynecologist, on whose research Freind's bill had been partially based.

The statement read, "He [Mecklenburg] regrets that his opinions were used to support Mr. Freind's position."

Freind called a press conference to respond. I began to feel a little better about the situation, about putting my name and my neck out for the story. The statement was to take place in the new Capitol media room, where it would be attended by a wide range of journalists and recorded for broadcast outlets. I felt vindicated by this turn of events, but still a little scared when I reached the door of the media room and found two big security officers guarding the entry. I flashed my press badge, and they opened the door for me. Inside, journalists from across the state filled the tables arranged in a semi-circle, facing the stage.

It hit me that I was perceived as being a strident woman who was overreacting to something the male journalists did not consider to be newsworthy. I pulled my shoulders up and walked to my front row seat, where Freind could not avoid seeing me as he took back his irrational statement. I looked around the room to see NBC News, all the media outlets from

Pennsylvania, and one news crew from Canada. The security guards closed the door and stood flanking the exit. *How ironic, I thought, the lawmaker who wanted to jail poor women, the man who threatened the lives and safety of women on welfare, felt threatened enough to bring protection to his press conference.*

Freind and members of his young staff stepped to the center of the stage, opened the microphone, and he spoke, expressing some regret for being "imprecise" with his remarks. He equivocated, refusing to say he had been wrong. Even when pressed, he would not take responsibility for his remarks. *No contrition!* This was not a retraction; it was a power-hungry legislator trying to walk back his overzealous claims. Nothing got my soul screaming like a loudmouth lawmaker trying to punish women who had no voice. When he opened the floor for questions, I asked him, "Did you not feel an obligation to check your information and verify it before making such a claim?" He glowered at me, knowing it had been my story that brought us to this press event.

"I've already responded to this," he yelled at me. Several other journalists re-asked the question, but he would not budge. He "regretted," he "was imprecise," but he would not admit he had been wrong.

I was shaking when I asked him the next question. "Don't you think your remarks are dangerous?"

He grabbed the podium with his fists and his face turned a deep red. He ignored me, pointing to a different reporter. Then he shut down the presser, telling us that if we wanted to know more, we could contact his spokesman. I'm sure I presented a confident front during the event and several of my colleagues praised me for forcing him to concede. But the truth was I felt very alone, sitting in a large room filled with almost all male journalists, some of whom had given me flack about covering the story. Even though I knew I had to speak for the women who had no voice–to raise questions, to point out the unfairness of a privileged man trying to incarcerate impoverished women–I was shaken by having to do so.

A few days after the press conference, I ran into Freind in the hallway of the Capitol Building and he walked over to me and shook his fist. The darkened hall was empty.

"I know what you're trying to do. You want to ruin my re-election effort, and I won't forget it either." As I stood there in the Rotunda, the huge dome over my head, I thought, *This man is trying to scare me. He's trying to shame me.* How condescending.

Then I began to feel the force of all the women whose lives had been sacrificed because they had dared to speak in halls of power. They were standing with me. *No,* I thought. *I am not going to be intimidated by this little man.* I shook my head at him, turned around and walked back to my office, thinking unsavory ideas about his election.

The experience had alarmed me. It stirred up an anger I didn't know lived inside me — a collective feeling, perhaps, shared by all women? I didn't sleep well for weeks. I watched over my shoulder as I walked to my car in the parking garage near the Capitol each evening. Every time I ran into the representative in the hallways of the Capitol, he scowled at me. But it didn't matter.

I had felt a personal connection to the women who had been

targeted by his legislation. I had become a foil for some of the men in the newsroom who were reluctant to cover the story, and the object of Freind's fury when I did so, making it crystal clear that not only was I walking with the oppressed, I was one of them. Like the women who would have been re-victimized by his bill, I felt besieged, as though the world was trying to take away something from me—a power that was rightfully mine. I understood just how, in the wrong hands, a story can be used to discredit and silence women. How it can be turned into a brush to paint us as worthless beings, undeserving of full citizenship. In the eyes of this chamber of power, poor women were not considered worthy of protection and I–as a woman with a voice and a small amount of power–had to struggle to have a seat at the news table.

My anger was deep, bottomless body deep. It flared in a subterranean place in me. Rather than hide it, I allowed the rage to open under its own force, and I reacted the way a sleeping goddess might, were she disturbed in her repose. Eventually, my anger boiled; then, it bubbled and transformed into something stronger. A sense of belonging to a sisterhood, a feeling of solidarity. These women were walking with me through weeks of fear and doubt, and I hoped that by speaking up, I'd revived my voice and the voices of those who were not able to speak in this chamber. Maybe I'd also cooked up the courage to continue searching for my own story.

Chapter 8

TRANSFIGURED

Southeastern Pennsylvania: 1998-2003

Fighting for the rights of women whose lives were threatened by lawmakers was one thing. Forging a path for women in journalism was another. My experience had brought me into direct contact with the white-hot flame of story's power and once touched by the heat, I knew I had to continue seeking my own story. Intuitively, I knew I was on the trail of a personal story that surpassed any I'd been told by my family.

After several years of working as a reporter, I enrolled in graduate school to study English Literature and Composition. I began at Pennsylvania State University, where the program was based on Rhetoric–material that reinforced argument and debate. The focus was counterintuitive to my desire to find a personal story, so I switched to another university, and a program with a specialty in Narrative Theory and Research. I longed to return to my love of story. And I yearned for the company of other women writers.

The works of Willa Cather, a journalist turned creative writer, fascinated me. Cather had been the target of other male writers, like Hemingway, who criticized her viciously. They questioned her personal life and her talent as an artist. Sylvia Plath, who foretold her own demise over the loss of her marriage in the lines of her poems. Emily Dickinson, who enchanted me with her insistence on seclusion, as well as her instructions: "Tell all the truth but tell it slant." But if I believed reading the works of these women was all I'd need to restore my voice and help me claim agency as a writer, I was wrong. A few classes into my program I realized, I was working in a field dominated by masculine rhetoric, an argumentative, linear style of expression. Very little space was given to nuanced, creative inquiry. The gaze and the voice were male. Privileged. Much like the tone I had experienced in the news industry.

I had come to immerse myself in stories, prose, and poetry written by women, to learn how my literary sisters had developed their craft but, what I found only reinforced the fact that women's voices were not regarded highly. Academia, which I began to call *"academenia"* seemed to want to oppress me more. Built on a patriarchal model of production, the goal was "publish or perish." Some of my female colleagues had internalized this oppression and, unable to break free of the constraints, turned on one another, competing and undermining each other's work.

Some of my graduate professors found me to be an unusual student. They were curious about me as a journalist turned intellectual who didn't quite fit into their world. Most had heard of me on the radio or seen me in news reports and they stamped onto me an impression of an opinionated, somewhat aggressive woman. I was an outsider who had somehow slipped into the ivory tower, past a gatekeeper who didn't notice that I was not a real academic.

Three years into my studies, I was allowed to teach some basic courses at the college level. Within a couple of years, I was given a full-time position, based on a combination of faculty and administrative duties. I even designed and won approval for a graduate certificate program in Composition Studies. But my status as an academic was still in question, at least in my mind. More troubling, I had to admit I was no closer to refining my voice as a story carrier, a writer of my family stories. In fact, after so much time in an academic setting, I worried that I might have moved further away from finding my authentic writing voice. Still, as is often the case, the story found me, demanding to be told in a new way.

Fifty years after losing my family, I wrote a dissertation for my doctorate degree, titled "Silence." Although based on a case study of women writers, I used the experience to explore ways to develop my own voice, to reclaim my worth as a woman writer. The final draft was based on the results of a year-long study conducted with six professional women writers, all published authors with advanced degrees in composition. One was an academic superstar in college in English studies, and she had been a mentor for me. Jacqueline Barton was the president of a highly prestigious professional organization, as well as an acclaimed journalist and writer, and I was grateful when she agreed to participate in my case study.

One Saturday morning, two years into my work, I sat down

at the local Perkins restaurant near the University with my committee and explained my thesis over breakfast.

"I want to begin with the question: 'How do external and internal pressures condition silence in women writers and how can silence be addressed?'" No one spoke. The waitress clearing the table behind us dropped a plate and uneaten blueberry pancakes spilled across the floor. Customers standing in line waiting for a table talked loudly. But, at my table, it was… crickets. One member of my dissertation committee, a youngish unconventional academic, new to the department, sat quietly, poking his over-easy eggs with toast tips. Finally, the head of the English Department, David, a heavy-handed but lovable Irishman, spoke up.

"And…you want to do this by asking participants to write personal stories? About their lives? I come to work to get away from personal stories. I'm not sure I want to read more of them." His eyes glistened as he flashed a condescending smile at me. David's pressed pale blue shirt seemed to stiffen, and his meticulously styled hair shone with gel. All signs to me of his awareness of his power.

See, I said to myself, *this is the attitude that keeps women from speaking or writing in a professional setting. Our stories are not important.* I could feel my face beginning to turn red.

David's colleague, Calista, a mature-aged woman I had worked with on several state and national writing programs, would not look at me. I stared at her, hoping she would speak or defend my idea, but disapproval seeped from her body as she sat, silently nodding at David's remark.

I thought, *The thick layers of hairspray holding Calista's 1960s pageboy hairstyle in place have probably frozen her brain and she cannot bring herself to disagree with David. She is stuck on his approval.* It wasn't kind of me to judge her appearance, especially while I was angry. But this was the central question of my research, my life. I wanted to know what kept women in the academy from speaking, as much as I wanted to understand the inability of women in my family to tell their stories. As we talked, it became clear that no member of the committee would challenge David. *After all, he was the boss, and what I was proposing to study might interfere with his notions of power.* How ironic to be met with silence for suggesting the idea of a study on the way women are silenced in the academy.

"More coffee?" the server asked. She bent over and filled everyone's cup. I quickly covered mine with my hand, refusing her hospitality. I wanted to have some control in this meeting, even if it was just over my coffee cup.

The break in the conversation gave David an out, so he moved on to talking about the weather becoming warm enough that he could get his boat out on the lake.

"Yes," Calista added, "My roses are blooming, so I know warmer days are on the way."

The new guy finished his eggs.

Jeez, I thought, *they have plenty to say about the weather. The weather! But not a word about the environment at our table–about the freezing cold air in our booth.* The waitress began to clear dishes from the table, and it was obvious that everyone was ready to end the meeting.

David picked up the check and gave me a final bit of advice. "Go back to the drawing board."

I lost my words, swallowed them in a surge of liquid that filled my mouth. The sour taste of betrayal. I wanted to spit at him. OK, that's awful for a grown woman to admit, but it was true. I wondered, *Why hadn't the one other woman at the table given me just a tiny bit of encouragement?*

Two weeks later, I asked Calista to step away from the committee. I admired her professionalism, but it was clear that she was uncomfortable with me. Perhaps my research focus made her question her own work. One day as we sat together over a lunch table in a café near the campus, I said to her, "We need to be realistic about this. You clearly do not like my research and I don't want our professional differences to hold me back."

I knew it was a bold thing to say, and I might be jeopardizing approval of my research, but I had to replace her with another faculty member with more progressive ideas about women. I had already lined up someone from another university, a woman who had advised me during my early graduate work. I had not come this far, read this many books, researched and written so many essays just to be silenced. This was my chance to learn how to help women—including me—revive our stories.

The next few months were spent researching the literature, focusing primarily on autobiography and memoir writers. Some of the authors I read had published theory and some wrote their personal stories. All of them, even the most successful, bumped into experiences that caused them to lose their writing voice. Virginia Woolf coped with a devastating depression that interfered with her work. Anne Morrow Lindbergh was censored by her marriage to a celebrity. Autobiographer Jill Ker Conway struggled to find the truth about her father's drowning, and, unable to locate his medical records, was left with unanswered questions about his manner of death. Fear, discrimination, lack of knowledge, religious beliefs, and societal notions about the value of women's stories all contributed to a pervasive experience of silence that seemed to paralyze women writers.

Finally, after multiple revisions, my proposal was approved. Honestly, I think the committee passed it through, hoping to get rid of me. Within a week I began to hold meetings with my study group. For over a year, we gathered to discuss our struggles to write. We wrote, shared our pieces, and learned from one another.

It is said that when the student is ready, the teacher will appear and that's what happened to me when one of the participants–the academic scholar I'd been so excited to welcome into the group–brought her personal stories to the table. Jacqueline had one of the most compelling stories I'd ever heard, one that would force me to confront my own prejudices and, as I worked with her, David's admonition about personal stories echoed in my mind. Several months earlier, I'd read Jacqueline's revelation that she'd had an affair with a graduate student in one of her classes at a well-known state university in the South, where she was the head of the department. I needed to understand this, to resolve my own questions about it before I could begin my work with her. I wanted to put off asking about it, but a couple of weeks into the study I wrote to her.

"Jackie, I have got to ask you, how did you process this experience? I mean, this is not supposed to happen in a classroom. It's the imbalance of power and all that. How did you come to terms with your decision to ignore or overlook your power as a professor and have an affair with a student?"

If I thought her response would help me understand her behavior, I was wrong.

"I married him," she wrote back. "We now have a daughter."

I was dismayed, didn't know how to respond to her. I wanted to lecture her. I wanted to tell her she had behaved unprofessionally. For weeks, I struggled with this information, wondering if I had an ethical obligation to honor Jackie, or her student, or the research. How was I going to write about this? Should I acknowledge it in my research and describe my personal reaction? I clearly couldn't condone her behavior but knew I had to suspend judgment long enough to think through my own feelings.

Jackie had been the reason I entered into the graduate program, and I admired her. Like me, she had been a journalist and nonfiction creative writer, who left her career to enter academia. I felt a professional connection to her but hearing her speak in this way made me feel like a voyeur, as though I'd entered a room where only secrets were shared. *Clearly*, I thought, *I'm out of my depth as a researcher.* I put the issue away and went forward with the research question: "What has silenced your voice?" For months, we exchanged messages from a distance and conducted telephone interviews about writing, her career, and the ways that she encountered resistance to her work as a highly successful academic — particularly from the men in her department.

At one point, she wrote to me. "I know what people say about me. That I'm too ambitious. That I publish too much, I have too much power." This was an experience I understood as well. I had also run into men in my department who seemed to want to compete with me or challenge me on my work. *After all, "academenia."*

"How has that affected your writing voice? Your agency?" I asked her.

"I feel I must do what I can to advance women. I owe my colleagues a good example as a professional, so I do my best and just try to ignore the remarks." I felt such compassion and admiration for Jackie. For months, we wrote, and I learned from her. Even if I still judged her on one level...

I wanted to square this image of the composed, intelligent woman with the teacher who violated what I considered to be a sacred boundary by seducing a student, so again, I wrote and asked her to help me see her reasoning. Weeks later, on a Saturday morning in September, I sat at my desk at home and opened my email messages. When I saw Jackie's name, I thought, *Oh, good. She's probably thought through her decision and she's writing to express contrition for betraying professional standards most teachers follow.* But as soon as I began to read, it was clear that she had something more important to tell me.

"I'm sorry for the delay in my response. I have leukemia and I've lost my vision. A friend is here with me, writing this message to you."

I was shocked. I read it again. "Did she say she has cancer?" I asked aloud. "Did she say she's blind and cannot see to write?" It didn't make sense and I said so to the walls in my office. "Jacqueline, the writer, the superstar of the discipline. She cannot write?" Then it hit me on a deeper level. *Jackie is dying. That's why she has written, to tell me she's dying.*

I stood up from my desk and walked into the living room. I paced across the room twice before sitting down on the white sectional in front of the large window, looking out across the sky. The bare branches of the pear trees reached upward, their long fingers like paintbrushes turning the sky a brighter blue. I watched long enough for fluffy clouds to move in, creating a contrast with the blue.

I had my vision. I could still see the world. Jackie did not. Her leukemia was going to kill her, just as it had taken my sister's life. The very idea struck me deeply, triggering grief I didn't know I was still carrying. I moved across the room, sat at the dining room table, and looked out at the vibrant maple tree whose crimson-colored leaves stared back at me. Their colors were so vivid, they seemed to speak. The scene was beautiful and tragic. Death and beauty. I needed to think before I could respond to her. Several days later, I sat down at my desk again and began to write. I knew my message couldn't be an academic one. I couldn't really talk about the study, nor her continued participation in it while undergoing cancer treatment.

How, I wondered, *could I honor her role in the study, while being present in her life as she traveled closer to death?* My disappointment in her behavior seemed so unimportant now. Or was it more important? I didn't know how to hold all of this and write a meaningful message back to her. I stood and walked across the room to the corner brick fireplace, needing warmth. In just a few weeks, fall would turn to winter. *Jackie might not live to see the seasons change*. Then I began to understand why she had been so willing to work with me. She had been carrying an untellable story and, on some level, perhaps unconsciously, she must have been searching for a safe place, where she could release it with someone who would honor her as a story carrier. Someone who would respond not as a writer or an academic, but as a witness to death.

"I'm never going to tell anyone about this," I said to the room. I knew that it was very likely that some of my colleagues were aware that Jackie's husband had been her young student, but I was not going to be the writer who put the story into print. The intimacy that had defined our working relationship was more important. So I decided to exclude this bit of information from the study. And I told myself David had been wrong about personal stories. He was dead wrong.

I went back into my office and wrote back to Jackie, expressing my sorrow for her illness. I thanked her for her courage in discussing her personal life. As I wrote, a new aspect of story carrying came to me. *Perhaps*, I thought, *some tales should be carried with more care than others. They should be told to a certain kind of listener, someone willing to witness the teller, and put aside judgment long enough to honor the dignity of the person sharing the experience.* I had put together this study and asked writers to share their stories. Now, I was being taught to be a witness, by listening deeply and responding with compassion.

Months later, my dissertation was approved. On a bleak

morning in December, I drove to western Pennsylvania to the university. There I stood in a procession line outside the graduation hall with fifty or so other candidates dressed in deep red gowns, ready to be awarded our degrees. My dissertation chair, who had become quite supportive of my work over the months, spotted me in line and approached. Frozen clouds painted the sky a gloomy gray.

"Did you know that Jackie lost her battle with cancer? She died four days ago," he said.

I shivered. I had heard the news that morning. "Thank you for letting me know." I couldn't find the words to express how I really felt about losing a sister who agreed to work with me and expose herself to criticism in the process. A woman with the courage to speak her truth. She'd only been sick for about six months, barely enough time to fight for her life.

We stood without speaking for another ten minutes and, although we both seemed to have more to say, neither one of us mentioned Jackie. I knew she'd be honored by the academic community, her name mentioned at the ceremony, and she would be the subject of articles about professional issues in education for months. I knew others would come forward to speak about their interactions with Jackie. She had established a path for women in academia, but she meant more to me than a list of achievements on a curriculum vitae. She had shown me how it looks for a woman to unsilence herself, to claim her agency. Weeks later, I thought of sharing the story I had been entrusted to carry about Jackie, but I could not do so.

After her death, I was haunted by the disclosure that she was the target of gossip by men in the department of the university where she taught and felt obligated to forever protect her privacy. I'm not claiming the moral high ground here; in fact, I think my decision to withhold details about her life was initially based on my early learning at my mother's knee, which taught me to follow a code of silence. But years later, I see my relationship with Jackie as something more important. It was a kind of preparation. Although I had been the researcher leading a study group, she had become my teacher, leading me to see something I might never have considered. Drawing something out of my soul that I needed to see. She taught me the importance of walking gently around the edge of a story, watching for the glimmer, as it slips across the soul into consciousness. I would carry hers in my heart with all my sisters who felt the sting of disapproval, even disappearance, through the imposition of silence. This had been precisely the lesson I needed before I could begin to write the stories carried by the women in my family, particularly those that no one wanted to talk about.

Chapter 9

LIFTED

Southeastern Pennsylvania: 2005

One summer morning as I got ready for a faculty planning meeting at the university to prepare for the fall semester, I put on my pantsuit, took out my grandmother's beads, and held them up in front of the bathroom mirror to see if they'd match. The necklace was made from delicate shells my grandmother bought on a trip to Hawaii years ago. My hands were still a little wet from brushing my teeth and when I tried to slip the hook into the clasp, the necklace slid through my fingers, crashing to the marble floor and breaking. Shells scattered everywhere.

"Oh no," I yelled. "I'm already late for work." I felt a shift in the room, as though the beads were trying to convey a message to me. Something in my life was going to break. Hurriedly, I gathered the beads and put them back into the little box with the cotton lining.

The next morning, I sat at the dining table, drinking coffee, trying to re-string the beads, and just as I was tying the knot, the phone rang. I dropped the necklace on the table and answered. It was my mother.

"Your grandmother passed away during the night," she informed me.

My heart jumped. My grandmother, who I called "Mommy," was my closest matrilineal relative, the matriarch of the family, and the only one I knew who had knowledge of the family stories.

"I'll come as soon as I can get a flight," I told my mother. I put the beads back into the box, rescheduled my classes for a week, and the next day, caught a plane to West Texas just in time to attend her funeral.

On the morning of her burial, Mommy's four daughters and one son gathered, along with several of her grandchildren, in a dusty dry cemetery outside Iraan, under a large white tent shading us from the blue sky, emptied of clouds by the West Texas wind. As we stood in the heat waiting for the minister to arrive, a local florist came walking across the sand, carrying a huge bouquet of white lilies.

"Oh, these are beautiful," I said, taking the flowers from him. All the flowers we expected had been delivered earlier and my mother and I had lined them around the silver-gray casket. I asked him, "Who sent these?"

"The card says they are from her brother, ma'am." I knew this was impossible or, at least, thought it to be untrue. As far as anyone knew, my grandmother was an only child. But I had to consider that she may have had family members that were unknown to us. None of our family knew much about her parents. We had never met them and were told they had abandoned Mommy when she was a little girl, leaving her with elderly grandparents. I had been told not to ask too many questions about her family as a child, but now, standing at her grave, I wondered why the story had never been told. Several more people began arriving to find seats under the tent, so I put my questions aside for a later time.

It was to be a short event. My mother and her sisters planned to stay only long enough to share a prayer in silence as her casket was lowered into the ground. Then, they'd gather the flowers and head to a nearby diner in Iraan for lunch. But I wanted more for Mommy. She deserved more than silence.

I waited until the minister had spoken and stepped forward, taking the microphone from him. I was determined to share my own story about my grandmother's life and the way she had inspired me to become a teacher, to love books. Now, she was prompting me from the grave to begin to question my life story. After I spoke, I invited others to share. They talked about her service as a beloved teacher, her work organizing the town's library, and her contributions as a historian and writer. All of it was lovely, but it was the story shared by her youngest granddaughter that touched me.

Janet, a twenty-something statuesque blonde, stood up in the last row, balancing her young baby on her hip. She began to share the memories of her visits to Mommy's house as a little girl. Janet called my grandmother by the name "Mee-maw." Her story, which I'll remember forever, was about soup. "Mee-maw always made the soup so hot; it was impossible to eat. So she'd tell us to sit very still for a long while, and to blow and blow on the soup until it cooled enough to take a bite." On the surface, this was an unremarkable reminiscence of a grandchild. But to me, it was much more. Her story took me back to my own childhood when I spent summers in Mommy's house living under her strict house rules.

Every afternoon in West Texas, as the sun grew intense, adults and kids sought out shady, cool spaces. Even the desert creatures found rocks to protect themselves from the heat. As children, we were told to find a quiet place in the house and sit very still and remain silent for what seemed like an eternity. Mommy closed the drapes in her living room and laid out mats of blankets on the floor for us to stretch out. We sat like little monks in a monastery. Then we'd lie down on the mats and eventually, with the sound of the large room fan rhythmically blowing air across us, we would begin to breathe deeply. In the dark, cavernous room, most of us fell asleep, while a couple would sit in silence for nearly two hours.

As a child, I thought this was a clever way for my grandmother to give herself a break for a few hours. But, as an adult, I saw it as a spiritual practice taught to her grandchildren. A lesson shared by a somewhat magical teacher, a wise woman who insisted that we learn to "get still" in the heat of the desert. To sit in the darkness in silence. Whether or not she meant to, she taught us to sit and to meditate. As an adult, I knew this as a common Buddhist practice called *anapanasati*, which was a ritualized form of sitting centered on the breath. I still practiced it, even though I'd never become good at sitting still for very long.

The stories carried by the grandchildren who stayed at Mommy's home over the years were pieces of glistening jewels, gifts passed down from one generation to the next. They were powerful examples of the ways lived experiences, when shared in stories, could take us beyond ourselves, just far enough to see things differently. They helped us to imagine a future that was beyond the often tedious day-to-day practices that made up our lives.

As the funeral service began to draw to a close, family members climbed into their cars and headed toward the tiny town of Iraan, where my grandmother had lived much of her life. I waited until all the cars left the cemetery. I opened the trunk of my car and pulled out the large set of colorful glass and metal wind chimes I'd purchased on my way to the funeral. I'd stood in the garden shop near my house in Pennsylvania, admiring the way the light reflected off the colored glass and decided I needed to pack the wind chimes into my suitcase, although I had no idea what I planned to do with them. My younger brother, Joseph, who had been driving, helped me carry the chimes and a large shepherd's hook to the grave. He dug beneath the layer of sand into the hard dirt, just deep enough to install the metal hook. We tested the stake for steadiness, then we added the chimes.

We stood, without speaking, watching the sun as it flashed through the pieces of green, orange, and blue glass. The wind began to pick up. I wondered what had prompted me to install wind chimes on my grandmother's grave, but I knew it had something to do with the wind and her untold story. I hoped the slender thread holding the chimes would not break. Walking back to the car, the wind began to sing. It was the sound of metal crashing into glass, creating high-pitched sounds. *Stories*, I thought. *The wind was picking up her stories*. I turned to look back, searching across the flat desert, hoping I'd catch a glimpse of the wind blowing across the earth. This morning, the wind felt different, less threatening to me, almost taking on the essence of an ally, a force with the power to carry forward the stories of my grandmother — the stories that remained untold, even at her death. As I opened the car door, I thought I heard my grandmother's name, "Wihelmina," whispered by the wind.

In the years following her death, several family members came forward with memories about her life in West Texas. Fragments of stories about her abandonment and disappearance. Pieces of stories I tried, over the years, to string together to build one solid narrative that would explain the legacy of the women in my family. But untold stories proved to be slippery, elusive, and difficult to repair when the thread carrying them had been broken.

Chapter 10

CARRIED

McCamey, Texas: 2005

I pressed the gas pedal down on the silver Ford, hitting the speed limit of eighty-five miles per hour. The car's V-8 engine was working hard to keep cool air coming out of the vents, to mediate the heat of the sun flashing through the windshield.

I had been driving for an hour and my mother and I had not spoken once. We were on our way to see her sister Deanna in Midland, Texas, the seat of the oil industry. I had planned to make a stop along the way, in the town of McCamey, to see my sister's grave. I turned to my mother, asking her if the cool air was too much for her. She looked so small in the oversized sunglasses she was wearing to protect her eyes from rapidly progressing macular degeneration. She barely nodded.

Driving along the open highway, the desert gave way to flat land on both sides, as far as I could see. It felt like we were crawling, and we hadn't seen another car for a long time. *Of course,* I thought, *it's ungodly hot and no one drives in the desert in the middle of the day.* Illusions of water puddles appeared, then disappeared as we seemed to get close to them. I saw something big in the distance and, before I knew it, we came across two huge black turkey buzzards hovering over a dead animal in the middle of my lane. They were the size of a very small compact car.

"Oh, my God." I laid on the horn, trying to frighten them away. One of the buzzards looked up but he didn't move away from his prey. He seemed to be staring directly at me, as though he wanted to give me a message. Swerving the car to try to miss them would be dangerous because they were apt to fly in any direction. I honked again. Finally, just as we got close, they both lifted off and flew up, barely clearing the hood of the car. "Hazardous birds," I yelled and honked several times again. I reached my arm across the seat, an automatic reaction, because I'd always been protective of my mother who seemed so much more vulnerable with age.

I was angry at her that morning. She had not been to the grave since Jeanie's burial, more than sixty years ago, and I had never seen it. I was angry at myself, too. The previous night, we argued over the visit. My mother insisted she didn't know how to find the grave where she had buried her daughter. I yelled back, "How could you not know this?"

"I don't know if I can do this. I'll have to call the mayor of the town and see if I can get a map of the grounds," she said. Apparently, only the mayor had access to burial information in the cemetery.

"I know, Mom, but we have to go." Why did she think of this as punishment? It was a mercy visit. She would finally see her child's grave, more than half a century after her death and I would, hopefully, release some of my rage and grief — hers and mine, which I had borne for years. "It will be hard, but we are not going to miss this opportunity," I said.

I wanted to cry, to yell at my mother, accuse her of neglect for refusing to honor Jeanie, for refusing to talk about her. For failing to help me cope with her loss. For holding Jeanie's loss as her tragedy alone, ignoring how I might have felt as a child too young to understand the death of the sister I loved. This was the anger, the resentment I had dragged around my entire life.

Half an hour later, I turned the car onto the paved road to enter the cemetery. The grounds were an oasis in the desert, a lush green grassy field, surrounded by a white rock fence and blooming red roses. I drove slowly as the pavement gave way to a gravel road. Down five, then ten rows of graves, to the middle. I parked the car near the shed. We got out and walked over to two caretakers. One of the men, who spoke broken English, knew we were coming, so he'd prepared a hand-drawn map, showing the lots with the names of both my sister and grandfather. I thanked him and he shook my hand.

"My sister *and* my grandfather?" Now I was yelling at my mother.

"Yes," she said. "They were buried next to one another."

"I never knew that!"

*My mother **had** been here in the past — she came home for her father's funeral and burial more than forty years ago, so she did see her child's grave. Why would she not tell me this?* We walked across the grass without speaking, my anger growing heavier with each step.

When we located the grave, it was unmarked. Unmarked.

What the hell? My grandfather, the family patriarch, had a large granite stone above his grave. The rock was engraved with his name, birthday, and death date. My sister's grave was bare. *So a child buried in the desert was exiled, forgotten, while the wealthy patriarch was honored.* My fury was almost too much to contain. I began to shake.

Something green moved in the breeze and I looked up to see a twenty-foot-tall green cedar tree over Jeanie's grave. I hadn't noticed it until we stood over the grave. A large, lush cedar, with blackish-green limbs, standing like a centurion.

"Look," I said, "She's protected by this big tree. Isn't that beautiful?" *How comforting that a tree had been standing guard over her all this time.* I reached out and touched a branch. "Feel this, Mom. It's soft."

My mother pinched her face as she wrapped her small fingers around the tip of one branch and I could feel the wall go up around her heart. She didn't respond. I wanted to be angry about that as well. I took a deep breath. Then, I stood very still and made the decision to remain silent. I had to consider just how much pain this trip caused her. I knew she was feeling both the loss of a child, the loss of her own childhood, and the years she had been unable to fully grieve. So in spite of my own anguish, I put my arms around her and pulled her close.

Silently, we walked back across the cemetery, passing the caretakers. We got into the car and drove back onto the desert highway, into the searing heat, watching for vultures hovering overhead. Mother, daughter, unspoken grief, all passengers.

I turned on the air conditioning and promised myself that

I wouldn't force her to say anything, even if it killed me. The fatigue on her face spoke to me of the exhaustion caused by years of carrying sadness and resentment, the emotions that a woman was expected to bear alone in a world that did not see her as a full person. A world that only appreciated her for her role as a mother. My mother's unspoken feelings–including shame, which had been carried in the darkness of grief across the years– felt heavier than granite. My feelings of anger were at a world that prioritized the death of an elderly family patriarch over that of a young girl. I decided to allow her the space and quiet, and I let the silence spread out between us like a soft blanket.

This is the part that broke my heart. Although at that time there had been no research linking cancer between mother and child, recent studies show cancer is caused by changes in the genes that control the way cells grow and multiply. Scientists have discovered hundreds of DNA and genetic changes, or mutations, which facilitate the development and spread of the disease. Cancer-related genetic changes can be triggered in the body at any time, even in the womb. Of course, no one would have blamed my mother for her daughter's cancer, nor would anyone have said my sister inherited the genetic changes in her cells that would allow it to grow in her body. But I knew of the way guilt builds a home in the hearts of mothers.

I had felt the impossible standard held over a mother's head, leaving traces of grief in the folds of the skin, behind the eyes, deep inside the womb, made heavier by a cancerous shame that one may never recover from. As I thought about this, my anger at my mother ebbed, giving way to anger at a world that had tortured her with the expectation that she bear this as her singular burden. An expectation so overwhelming, it had split mother off from her daughter. From both daughters. Considering how we had both been silenced, I decided to continue — at least for one more day — to carry her grief, her rage, and my own for a little longer.

Pennsylvania: 2008

Years after visiting my sister's grave, I began to understand how the emotional traces of my sister's illness and death took root in my DNA, shaping my life and those of my own children and their children in unique ways. The cancer narrative that first appeared in my family, taking my sister's life, arose again in the life of my grandson. My son's youngest son, Luke, was diagnosed with ALL at age eleven–the same form of leukemia that had ended Jeanie's life. The disease had jumped a generation to appear in Luke's life. At first, no one seemed to remember my sister's diagnosis. At least, not right away. We were all very focused on Luke's health. He endured more than three years of brutal chemotherapy, moving close to death before returning to the door of remission. He was eventually declared cancer-free. At the same time, and no one could have anticipated this, Luke's condition triggered something in my mother's mind — a memory she had been unable to feel for decades — her own child's illness and death. It was as if she was given permission to remember her own loss. She began to send cards to Luke every week, cards with pictures of cats because he loved them. She flew from Texas to Pennsylvania to see him.

And, finally, my mother and I began to talk about my sister.

Southeastern Pennsylvania: 2012

One chilly winter afternoon, I decided to push my mother for more information about Jeanie's illness. I took my phone upstairs to my haven and called her. She was still healthy, and her mind was clear at that time. The conversation did not begin on a pleasant note.

"Did you know that when Jeanie was in the hospital, your father was having an affair with one of her nurses on the ward?" The shock took my words away. I didn't know what to say. "We were at the Children's Hospital in Dallas, and I found them together in another room."

My God! I cannot believe my ears. Did she say my father was…? "Oh." It felt as though someone punched the word out of my throat. "How did this happen?"

"The nurse invited us to stay at her house overnight and, thinking it was a kind gesture on her part, we agreed to do so. I woke up in the middle of the night and your father was gone. I walked into the living room and found them together." Hearing this about my father brought up more questions about his disappearance from my life. Now my mother's decision to divorce my father shortly after Jeanie's death made sense to me.

No wonder, I thought, *I had carried a need to protect her. Something in me must have known how she'd suffered in her marriage.* She noticed my silence and suggested that we change the topic.

"Let's talk about something else," my mother said. "We were talking about Jeanie." I was glad to move away from the news of my father's betrayal. I'd had enough difficulty coming to terms with his loss and was not ready to complicate things.

"Mom, I know I was just a toddler when she died, but Jeanie lived on in my soul for many, many years. I remember the way she held me as a tiny child." Even as I spoke, I began to worry she'd say I was still imagining things. This had always been her complaint about my recollections–that I had a "wild imagination," or she'd accuse me of "holding onto everything." But this time it was different. She didn't try to stop me. She let me speak and, moved by my words, my mother began to cry.

"Oh! I had no idea. I am surprised to hear that you remember her so well." I had been prepared to be accused of being silly or worse. This was not that. *What had changed that allowed her now to believe I could have such a powerful memory?* We talked more, about how it felt to lose a child at the age of twenty-four, about how sweet her oldest daughter was, how she was adored by everyone in the family. It was as though a new chapter of our story as mother and daughter was unfolding; the story was changing direction and my mother's remembrances of her little girl finally began to rush out in her words. She was becoming unsilenced.

At one point in the call, she asked if I would like to have some of Jeanie's possessions and promised to send me some of the baby dresses she'd saved. A few weeks later, a small box arrived, and I took it to my bedroom to unpack and inspect the contents. A tiny, smocked baby dress with a ruffle around the collar and Jeanie's name embroidered on the front. A small baby blanket. A baby book with a faded green cover, filled with memories of my sister's early years. Her medical records and death certificate. Several sepia-tone photographs of Jeanie as a healthy young girl, before she became ill. In each photograph, Jeanie wore a ribbon in her hair—placed, I'm sure, by my mother. As I held the pieces to my heart, I began to feel the story of her life materialize. I was holding evidence of the story that had been buried in my soul for years. A story I had been forbidden to tell for most of my life.

I tried several times over the years to move back to West Texas but was not able to tolerate the wind and heat for very long, so I returned to Pennsylvania. Perhaps I needed the distance from the desert to find my story. Perhaps I needed the trees.

Shortly after re-marrying for the third time, my husband and I bought a house on the edge of the Appalachian Forest, filled with eastern hemlock, red sugar maple, flowering dogwood, pin oak and red oak, and a wide variety of pines. I measured my life in seasonal changes in the woods, from the black, barked structures, tracing pencil-thin lines into the flannel-gray winter sky, to the pollen-laden, spring branches relentlessly stretching toward the blue canopy overhead, opening into leaf-swollen trees in a range of sublime shades of green in the summer. Trees offered me solace from the harsh memories of the desert, showing me how to dig my toes into the earth and remain steady through each phase of life. Day after day. Season after season. Year after year.

Although I still visited Texas, I could not be away from the forest for long and often cut short my visits to return home, where trees sustained hope for me. When I thought about my sister, I was reminded of the tall cedar tree that stood over her grave, nourishing her soul with heartbeats transmitted across an unseen threshold. And I thought about the way my mother and I were united by a grief journey as carriers of her untold story.

Chapter 11

DEPARTED

Great Falls, Montana: 1970

My lifelong search for my family's narrative taught me a lot about the nature of stories. Some did not want to be told and stubbornly withheld their details until the one carrying the tale was willing to surrender, yield control, and let the tale disclose itself to the world. Some were too dangerous to be told and had the wisdom to hide until it was safe. I discovered that some stories kill. It took me a long time to understand this and if it seems hard to believe, consider the tragic tale of my aunt's life.

In the mid-1970s, my mother's sister Deanna lived west of Iraan, in the oil boom city of Odessa. Midland-Odessa was home to one of the biggest success stories of the oil industry, where, although the cost to the environment was immeasurable, the Texas oil legacy lived on, as a major component of the national economy and a cultural force. Roughnecks still slung cables and pipes on big rigs. The smell of oil still hung in the air. And a wildcatter somewhere continued to search the earth for black gold, drawn by the fantasy that somewhere underground, invisible to the naked eye, was a magical substance. All of it a dream that anything could happen in this land, and it could be fantastic, or it could be deadly.

In 1970, I didn't know much about my mother's life. I didn't know she'd grown up in a home with a father who was absent until she was six years old. Not much about her childhood had been shared with me, so I had no idea how this had shaped her life, nor that of her younger sister, Deanna. The story of the sisters was not revealed until much later in my life, so I didn't have any knowledge about the dangerous story they were carrying.

Born second in her family, Deanna was my favorite aunt — so intelligent, reserved, and serene. On the surface, her life as an adult appeared to be normal, but, unbeknownst to me, she had been taught to ignore danger. So perhaps she missed the signs that might have revealed its presence. Several years into their marriage, her husband, a well-known city official in Odessa, engaged in an extramarital affair and, at one point, left her for another woman. A few months later, he left his second wife when he suspected she had been unfaithful to him. Then, one evening, he broke into her home and shot and killed his second wife and the man he discovered in her bed. He then turned the gun on himself. All three died.

At the time, I was living in Great Falls, Montana with my first husband in a third-floor apartment in an old, stately home. The news of the murder-suicide came to me on a December morning, as I sat at the writing desk in the living room, watching the snowy scene outside the window. Delicate flakes fell across the sky, landing noiselessly on the ground below.

The phone rang. My mother's voice on the other end. She was calling me from Texas with the news of my uncle's death. "No one is talking about this," she cautioned me. She began to whisper. "Your uncle was not himself—he was distraught." She told me about the double-murder-suicide in a matter-of-fact way, but I could hear undertones of shame in her voice.

"God, Mom. Is Deanna safe? Is she ok?"

At first, I wondered how my mother could talk about tragedy with so little emotion, but it hit me that she had always spoken this way about the most significant and heartbreaking events in the family. She would never raise her voice or cry out in pain. Never.

"What do you mean, 'he wasn't himself?' When did he become someone who would take lives?" My mother spoke about him as though he'd come down with a fever and turned into a killer overnight. I was stunned and confused. "Mom, I want to come home," I said.

She wanted to end the phone call.

"I'll write you a letter with more information," she promised, and we hung up. I sat back down at the desk, staring outside at the snow-filled sky, wondering how many flurries it would take to fill in the emptiness in my soul. Ten days later, her letter came, and I opened it, expecting to get some hint, some explanation of this story of tragic loss in my family. But what I got was a clinical sentence. "Several weeks after the shootings, Deanna announced she had forgiven her husband, defending his actions as so uncharacteristic that he could not be blamed for his crimes."

I began to yell as I read. "Uncharacteristic?" I wondered if he had given signs of the existence of a deep-seated potential to commit harm. Or, had my aunt been unable to see the signs, to recognize them because she had been taught to live with cruelty from a man? I put the letter down and called my mother. "Why didn't you call me with this?" I asked.

She was dismissive. "You are living so far away and can't do anything to help. There was no need to upset you."

As we spoke, I began to understand that no one in my family saw the connection between the suffering my aunt experienced as a young girl—abandoned by her father—and her marriage to an abusive man who turned into a murderer. This was considered a singular tragedy, an isolated incident, not related to a larger family narrative. No one saw this as an outworking of the unspoken residue of loss that had coated the hearts of the sisters. Unseen, the story existed somewhere in Deanna's soul, leaving her unable to protect herself. She had been blinded by the silence. Yet, I thought there had to be more, a bigger story than anyone knew.

That afternoon, I sat in front of the window, waiting for my husband to return home, watching the world turn darker, as I thought about evidence. I began to compare Deanna's story to my own story of disappearance, wondering if the two were related. No evidence had existed that I was removed and hidden from my father as a child, and I suspected that any evidence that an ancestor in my family had been married to a violent man, if it existed at all, would not have been acknowledged. I wondered how many other secrets were being held in the family. Had there been signs that might have alerted my aunt to danger? If so, where were they? The silence in my family was beginning to be alarming, unsettling. I shivered, thinking about the possibilities. But it would take many more years for me to fully comprehend the force of the family legacy of abandonment, and to understand how it linked the story of Deanna's tragic marriage to my own.

Southeastern Pennsylvania: 2006

Many years after divorcing my first husband, I remarried. My sons were grown and had begun to have families of their own. I had invested several years in therapy and my own growth and, although I knew I hadn't resolved all the knots carried over from my childhood, I wanted to try marriage again. A few years into my second marriage, I returned to graduate school and earned a doctorate degree. But within two years of my graduation, I began to have vague feelings of discomfort about my marriage. My husband Mark, who struggled with depression, hit a very difficult time in his life. He lost his job — a high paying position — and he began to feel uncomfortable with my professional success and growing independence. In fact, he became hurtful and abusive. I left him. I returned to him. We spent months spiraling downward as a couple and I became worried about his stability. I even convinced him to visit a therapist with me.

One afternoon in the therapist's tiny, sun-filled office, I sunk down into an overstuffed leather corner chair, listening to the burbling fountain next to her desk. It was early autumn, and the sun created a prism when it hit glass chimes hanging on her window. I had called her the day before, asking for an emergency appointment. She agreed to meet with both of us when I expressed my concerns.

As soon as we sat down, I immediately voiced my fears, speaking directly to Mark. "I'm worried that you'll hurt yourself." I believed saying this to him, with a witness, would encourage him to be real with me. He uncrossed his legs, leaned his head back on the wall, and did the oddest thing. He smiled at me but did not answer. "Do you promise me that if you are planning to do something dangerous, you'll come to me?" I continued. He still didn't respond.

I grew frantic, twisting my wedding rings, my neck growing stiff from the stress that was building in my body. *Why didn't the therapist speak to him?* I wondered. *Couldn't she see how worried I was?* I looked at her with dismay written across my face. *Couldn't she say something?*

Finally, she did begin to speak, engaging Mark in a conversation, and we talked for another hour. I was growing more upset. Then she advised me, "Go home and stop worrying about him. He'll get over this." She must have seen the shock on my face. "You, however, need to relax. You need to free yourself from the worry you're carrying for him."

We left the tiny office and drove to a nearby restaurant. I ordered a glass of wine. Then another. *Clearly, I had to release this.*

For the next two days, I left the house early in the morning to go for a run. *Perhaps the therapist was right. I needed to be more optimistic.* Several days later, I got out of bed and went into the kitchen to pour a cup of coffee. Mark was loading the dishwasher.

"What are you doing?" I asked.

He smiled. The October sun filled the room, and I knew it would turn into a beautiful day. Anyway, I didn't have time to ask too many questions. I had to teach three long classes and wanted to get to the campus early to make photocopies of handouts. I dressed, grabbed my books and student essays, and kissed him goodbye on the way out the front door.

During the afternoon, something tugged at me, causing me to lose my concentration. It was during my second class, a one-and-a-half-hour-long session, when it hit me. I was standing in front of the computer-filled classroom, instructing students on a research assignment. *Something's wrong,* I thought. Without finishing my sentence, I told students I had to leave the room and would return. I stepped out into the small, dark hallway with my cell phone and dialed my home phone number. No answer.

That's odd. He should be home at this time.

I dialed again and left a message. "Mark, I'm on a break in my class. I'll be home in a few hours. Just want to check to see if you need anything."

I lied, even to myself. I was worried—no, I was afraid. *Why hadn't he answered the second call?*

In between classes, I ran to my office on the second floor and called again. Then I returned to teach the next class. Two or three more times that afternoon, I called the house. Each time I left messages when no one answered. Finally, fifteen minutes earlier than usual, I dismissed my last class and gathered my books.

"Uh, see you next week. I'm in a hurry," I told them. "Email me if you have questions." They looked somewhat confused because I always allowed time at the end of class to respond to their questions. Not tonight. It was growing late, and I was in a hurry to get home.

I flew across the large student-faculty parking lot behind the building, passing by students on the way. One tried to stop me to talk, but I told her, "I can't speak now. I've got to get home."

I spun my new black car across the back roads, where I could drive fast and avoid heavy traffic. I opened the moonroof and saw right away the full orb staring at me. "What?" I yelled at the sky.

I called home again. No answer. I left another message. "Damn it, Mark, pick up the phone. I've been trying to call you all afternoon."

Then, in a panic, I called my daughter-in-law to ask if she or my son had heard from him. They hadn't.

"I've been trying to reach him from the classroom for hours." I tried to hide the fear in my voice. "Oh well, I guess he's gone out for a beer." I pushed the pedal harder, driving a bit faster and looked up at the sky, filled with twinkling stars, all dancing as though to a song. *What is it?* I wondered. *What do they know?*

We lived in a sedate, settled neighborhood, filled with lovely homes, a quiet part of town where families retired early in the evenings. As soon as I turned the corner to my street, I sensed the difference in the energy — the air was charged with danger, and I became frantic. It was dark when I approached my house; I could see that it was the only one on the street with no lights. Not even the front porch light had been turned on.

"What the hell!" I screamed.

I turned my car into the driveway, not even bothering to

open the garage door as I usually did. I jumped out and ran to the front door, leaving the car door open. On my way to the door, I waved to my next-door neighbor, who wished me a good evening as he carried his trash can to the front of his house. As soon as I put the key into the lock, I felt it. A shift in the universe. Something was different on the other side of the door, the one I had walked through for ten years. It was a different house.

Everything was dark inside, so I began to turn on the lights as I ran from room to room. Then I went into the kitchen, where I found his body on the floor.

"Mark, Mark," I screamed.

I knelt on one knee to touch him, but it was apparent that he was dead. I looked up quickly, wondering if someone was in the house, wondering what had happened to him. None of it made sense. There was no sign of a problem, no blood. Nothing. All of a sudden, I felt something, a presence–an energy moving across the room toward the open window. I shuddered. I sat for a moment, wondering if I'd be able to move, to do anything. Then I screamed. I ran back through the living room, out the front door, yelling for my neighbor.

"Chuck! Help me. Mark is dead."

Chuck dropped his trash can and ran across the yard. "Where is he?"

I pointed inside the house and Chuck ran in to find him.

Eventually, the police came. An ambulance came. Detectives came and one walked me down the street to a neighbor's house so they could do their work outside of my presence. I cannot truthfully say I was surprised, but I was shocked. Shaken.

Traumatized. It's not that I didn't see warning signs because I had felt impending danger for weeks. He had been fired from his job and became darkly morose. But I did not understand the importance of trusting my own intuition. It was not until several days later when my sons took me back to the house that I was able to see the evidence of what had happened to him. Perhaps in the initial shock, I missed it.

For ten years after Mark's death, I insisted that he had not taken his life. That someone had come into our home and murdered him. The police detective in charge of the case was very gentle with me when I protested and demanded a bigger investigation. I argued with everyone as I tried to come to terms with reality. Finally, I had to accept what I had not allowed myself to know. Ironically, it was my mother, the one who had schooled me in silence, who helped me to see this awful truth.

We spoke on the phone about a week after my husband's death. She didn't mince words.

"He cut his throat. How can you not see this?"

I couldn't believe her insensitivity, her use of the word *suicide*.

"No, don't say such a thing. He did not!" I said.

She dug in her heels, imploring me to release my denial.

"He's a murderer," she said.

"How can you be so cold? So cruel to me?" I yelled back at her.

I looked out the large dining room window at the tiny white lights my son and I had strung across the big sweetgum in the back yard two days ago. Mark's death had plunged me into a state of bewilderment, where I believed anything was possible. Anyone could vanish. And re-appear. On one level, I believed the lights would signal to my husband that I was waiting for him to come home.

"Mother," I begged. "Come up here. I need you."

I needed my mother to hold me and explain why this story had appeared again in my family. When I thought back to my uncle's murder-suicide so many years earlier, I felt a chilling sensation — a familiarity — as though there was a story I was carrying in my bones. The man had disappeared, but the story remained.

At the time, I had not understood my aunt's rush to forgive her husband for his crime. But the horror of my own husband's suicide had taken away my words, leaving me in denial. Without words to contain the feelings, I, too, began to lose my ability to see the truth. That's what a story can do to the soul.

I knew it would be helpful if I could write about my loss, so I began to try to write about Mark, about our marriage, about his suicide. Each time I sat down at my desk to compose, the words seemed to slip away, and, quickly, I fell into a deep grief. Writing was painful. Remembering was torturous.

Six months after his death, on a blustery November night, a friend talked me into going to a writing workshop. Thinking it might help me to write in a group, I agreed to go with her to the library in Lancaster, Pennsylvania, where we'd join other writers from the area. Twenty of us gathered around the table. There were bearded poets, tunic-wearing writers with dangling earrings and beaded necklaces, and memoirists clad in loose gauzy dresses. We were anxious to begin our work. We learned in and listened to the leader's prompt.

"Tell a story in fifteen minutes," she said, offering no other explanation.

I sat, staring at the knots in the old, oversized oak table, raised my pen over my journal, and wondered how I'd begin to tell the story about my husband, who was stabbed to death in our home. Suddenly, the room felt very small, crowded with other writers who had stories to tell. For a moment, I couldn't breathe. I became very still, listening to the wind blowing dry leaves in the street, waiting for inspiration to write the story about a phantastic life filled with people who disappeared.

Chapter 12

REVIVED

Southeastern Pennsylvania: 2018

It took years to feel safe again after Mark's death. The unspeakable horror of it plunged me into a prolonged period of grief and depression and when I finally came up for air, I suffered with nightmares, fear of being hurt or killed myself, and the realization that the shock of his suicide had torn apart my family. My youngest son was angry at me. My relationship with my grandchildren felt broken. My oldest son seemed to resent me. I was not sure I'd ever survive the loss of everyone.

Gradually, after years of grief therapy, I began to walk across a new threshold, leading me into a different way of life. I finally accepted that I was a widow, and the role opened portals to new realms, new ways of being in the world. Eventually, I felt free to write again and this time, I did so in a much different way. I began to trust my intuition to lead me to stories that were held deep within my body, where I encountered people and experiences I had never known to exist. Some of it felt otherworldly, as I began to feel the presence of ancestors and others who had been lost to me for so many years.

How did I get here? Perhaps it was the cumulative effect of prolonged shock. Perhaps, as my mother had always insisted, I "had a wild imagination." Either way, I felt a new freedom to explore and live a very different kind of life. After seven years, I re-married a loving man with a gentle soul.

Two years into our marriage, I enrolled in seminary, where I studied spiritual direction. My supervising professor, a female pastor from the area, introduced me to ancient faith practices of spirituality, including Celtic Spirituality and the Ignatian Exercises — a kind of spiritual journey following the life of Jesus by entering into prayers, meditation, reflections, and directions, which rely heavily on the imagination. In this setting, my ability to release control and allow myself to believe in the supernatural was rewarded and praised. My mentor in the program was particularly encouraging when it came to writing my life story.

After seminary, I began to explore other faith traditions, studying Buddhist, Islamic, Hindu, and Indigenous spiritual practices, focusing on the gods and goddesses in each one, as well as stories of creation and redemption. I enrolled in several online courses on interfaith beliefs, which opened new horizons for me. During this season of my life, I began to see dramatic changes in my writing, as I expanded into poetry, studying haiku and exploring in more depth the use of imagery and metaphor. While enrolled in one course in particular, I tested a concept that opened me up to even deeper levels of creating.

It was the winter solstice and, in my part of the country, the longest night of the year. We were living through a worldwide pandemic, and I could do little more than study and write. I spent most of my evenings in my home office, enveloped in sienna-colored walls, glowing from the candle burning on my desk. One evening sitting at my desk, I peered over the top of the laptop computer at the black sky, barely paying attention to the speaker in the Zoom class that had begun an hour ago. I was losing interest in the lecture and wondered if I should leave the meeting.

The sound of a woman's voice called me back into the classroom. She was speaking through my headphones in a heavy foreign accent. For two weeks, I'd immersed myself in this course, studying spirituality based on personal experience with the divine, often the divine feminine. We'd been reading legends and tales of the great goddesses from other faiths who possessed a kind of wisdom that's not often shared in Western culture. Their dramatic tales of supernatural powers inspired me.

The speaker, a Tibetan Buddhist nun, talked about the Hindu goddess Kali. "She is the most fierce and powerful Hindu goddess, often pictured holding the severed head of a demon she has slayed. Considered the most frightening and strongest mother figure of the universe, Kali is capable of restoring balance when the world feels out of order."

"This," I said to myself, "is the kind of heroine I need to rescue me from the confusion of my life." Years of bad marriages, lost relationships, and a childhood history that still kept me awake at night called me to make sense out of my life, to find a way to create an enduring legacy out of the turmoil. I turned my attention back to the speaker and was immediately captivated by the next entity she described: the *dakini*, a "divine feminine essence, much revered in the Tantric tradition, as a carrier of wisdom." She showed colorful slides of the *dakini*, a dark-skinned wraithlike sprite, covered in silky shawls that seemed to fly away from her body as she soared across the horizon. Around her neck was a chain of tiny skulls and jewels, a glittering crown sat atop her head, and she held a long metal sword above her body as she moved.

My eyes focused on the images as the instructor said, "She is the most sacred aspect of the feminine principle in Tibetan Buddhism, embodying both humanity and divinity in feminine form."

But what grabbed my attention was that she lived in space. She had no home. Known as *khandro*, the sky dancer, she flew through clouds, pummeling the high winds fearlessly. Several days earlier, I had read about the *dakini*, as described by feminist theologian Meggan Watterson, who explained, "The *dakini* has left the rigid boundaries of Earth and the laws of gravity. She is about the limitlessness of the sky."

As I listened to the lecture, and thought about the concept of space, it occurred to me that perhaps I had lived too long in this hemisphere, in a body that has been bound by rules of oppression that have restricted my imagination. This idea, this essence of a feminine principle freed from the constraints of a powerful system, was exhilarating.

I wondered, *Could I call on the essence of the* dakini *to help me?* After all, as a child, I had lived in what seemed to be a limitless horizon, a desert so open I was unable to find a way to feel safe. *Perhaps stories also existed in another realm, nourished by an energy I did not understand.* My mind was blown by the idea that I might be able to appeal to a goddess to lead me beyond the tale of loss I had been telling. To see my childhood abandonment in a new way. *Perhaps a supernatural warrior woman could guide me into a new literary genre, where a bigger, more expansive story was waiting to be discovered. A new genre.* Besides, calling on the *dakini* would give me a metaphorical bridge for initiating a dialogue with my ancestors — my mother, my sister, my father, my grandmother — in a new and different way, by reaching across the threshold that bound me to the earth. I was eager to try this method. Admittedly, this was driven by the desire of a little girl who was desperately seeking her story, but it might also help me find a divine source for growing wisdom out of the original wound.

Chapter 13

OBSCURED

Terlingua, Texas: 2017

My husband, Larry, held my hand as we stood at the entry of the graveyard in Terlingua, Texas, a ghost town that sits on the border of Texas and Mexico. From what I could see through the rock arches, I wasn't sure if I wanted to enter or get back into the car and go home.

We had come to find my father's grave–some forty years after his death. He died in 1974, but I didn't know this until more than a year later, when my mother decided to share the news. She was visiting me in Pennsylvania where I lived with my first husband and two small sons. We had just put the boys to bed and were sitting in the kitchen, drinking herbal tea, watching the sky turn a deep blue, as the sun kissed the tops of large oak and maple trees in my backyard. I got out a tin of homemade almond biscotti wafers and brought them to the table.

Before I could sit down, she began. "Your father is gone."

She must have seen the surprised look on my face. *She had never called him "my father."*

"What happened?" I asked.

"Apparently, it was his heart. My mother read about his death in the newspaper a year ago, but she didn't let me know until recently," my mother said.

I opened the tin of biscuits, gave my mother a napkin, sat down, and looked out the window at the vegetable garden, just beginning to sprout carrots. It was in the corner where, earlier in the day, my two-year-old stood, barefooted, picking up mulberries that had dropped to the ground, from the tree whose branch draped over the fence.

"Umm..." he said, when he saw me, stuffing his little mouth. I carried a cup of orange juice as a bribe to pry the berries from his fingers, hoping to stave off a rebellion. His beautiful face was stained deep purple and framed by his long dark locks. The face of a child who did not yet know of loss beyond berries. I was no longer surprised by delayed news of death in my family, but it hit me in the gut when I remembered my son standing in the garden. A sight my father would never see.

"Can you imagine?" my mother said. "Keeping this from me for over a year?" My jaw dropped. *My mother, the diva of secrets, shocked by her mother's failure to disclose a death.* We dipped our biscuits in the tea.

Now, at the cemetery, my husband tugged on my arm. "Let's just walk inside. We don't have to stay if you're not comfortable."

"It looks so desolate." Stacked rock columns, topped with ornate metal crosses framing a vista of desert backed up by distant mountains. The cemetery, on the National Register of Historic Places, is often described by visitors as "eerie and quirky." I was not even slightly amused by one travel writer's description of it as a "destination graveyard."

Had my husband not encouraged me to look for it, I would never have come this far to find a man whose disappearance remained unexplained to me. I still struggled to know whether he had left us or my mother had divorced him and told him to leave. It was another untold story. When we had arrived in Terlingua, known as a mecca for eccentric artists, musicians, and those seeking to drop out of the world, we stopped at the old general store for information.

The clerk who sold us T-shirts splashed with "Terlingua, Ghost Town" took our credit card and bagged the souvenirs. Then, she pulled a cigarette out of her shirt pocket, lit it, and began to share the graveyard's history. "Everyone comes to photograph this cemetery. Most of the people buried here were miners who worked for the defunct Chisos Mining Company, located right next to the cemetery. They all died from mercury poisoning," she said.

I felt a slight cramp in my stomach. We thanked her and left; then we walked around the little town, taking photos of the old courthouse, remains of the jail, and the Starlight Theater Restaurant and Saloon, all set against the backdrop of Big Bend National Forest on one side and the desert land bordering Mexico on the other.

I was not sure about continuing this search after the clerk's description. Before the trip, I had read that most of the dead could not be buried in the ground because it was too rocky, so their bodies were laid to rest under mounds of stone. Still, I told myself I could try to hold this horrific information, along with the grief that rose in my throat–residual trauma carried by the little girl whose daddy had disappeared so many years ago. My brother, Jon, had given me photos he took of the grave when he found it, fifteen years earlier, so I knew what to look for: a large mound of rocks marked by a vibrant blue cross with my father's name inscribed on it. I was sure I'd have no trouble finding it.

Larry squeezed my hand, suggesting that we split up and begin to search the rows, meeting in the middle.

"Ok, I'm ok," I told myself. Maybe dividing this up into a manageable search would make it easier. Reluctantly, I walked into the dusty barren lot, filled with about two hundred graves. The grounds were an unkempt field, with creosote bushes overspreading the graves. A few were marked by granite headstones, some broken. Most, however, had only weather-worn handmade wooden crosses, blown over by the heavy winds, and, if names had once been present, they were no longer visible. Some graves were outlined by rows of empty bottles, others peppered with broken glass holders, spent candles, incense bowls, and stacks of coins. Framed photographs of loved ones: a small child, a beloved grandfather. Decorations left by last year's Dia de Los Muertos visitors, strewn everywhere. Crepe paper blew around the base of a large cross. Relics bursting through the barriers of time and space, blending the past with the present.

I was drawn deeper into the boneyard, walking back and forth through the unmarked rows in my sandals. The cactus pricked my feet, like tiny fingers scratching my skin. The sand seemed to be heavier on the ground inside this yard, the rocks, too. Suddenly I began to feel the density of lives that had been lived, their stories now encased, held deep within their shrunken bones. I slowed down, walking gently, allowing myself to take in the energy emanating from the ground. I didn't want to disturb the stories.

The wind howled; a metal-sour taste filled my mouth. I turned to search the sky for birds, but nothing seemed to live in the vast blue except chunky, thick, white clouds. A gust knocked me back a bit and I began to listen. *Buzz. Whoosh. Moan.* Behind me, a flash of movement. I turned around, but nothing was there. Here felt like there. Now felt like then. A magnetic force pulled me down, then up. Voices of ancestors seemed to be speaking to me. This was a world with no distinction between one time and another.

I stopped in the middle aisle and looked up into the sky. The clouds seemed to thin out and I could almost see my mother talking with me as a five-year old girl whose father had left. I was crying and pleading with her.

"Where is my daddy? I want to see him," I scream.

She glares at me. She doesn't reach out or hold me. She doesn't answer at first. Then, "Huh! He doesn't love you. He'd be here if he did."

Crying, I yell back. "That's not true. Where is he? Where is Jeanie?"

These were the questions that I carried deep in my bones all my life. Questions that, with no answers, would remain.

I had never known why my father left, whether it had been his choice, or if he left because my mother divorced him. For years, I had been confused about why he'd never tried to find me, never tried to rescue me. When I'd asked, I had been given conflicting explanations. My mother's family told me that he wanted to live his life free of responsibilities.

Many years later, when I finally was able to locate one of his cousins, she told me my father had searched for me and was kept away by my mother and stepfather. She added that he died of a broken heart over losing his children. Not knowing the real story was heartbreaking and it compounded my anger at my mother.

Behind me, Larry called out to me, and I turned around to find him, standing at the back of the graveyard by a chain link fence. When I got close, he wrapped his arm around my shoulders. We stood for a few minutes, staring at the scene before us, the abandoned mine, still an open pit. The fence around it, a border that symbolized the loss of what was once familiar to me — my father and my sister, my family. On one side was the life I had created for myself out of the remains of loss. On the other side of the deep pit, a land foreign to me. As foreign as the memory of the child who had been abandoned. I realized I had been standing at the threshold of two different worlds, the familiar and the no-longer-familiar, the spiritual and the material. The wall separating us felt very thin and I reached above me, into space, believing I could touch something solid. A rock. A cross.

Larry motioned me back toward the entrance, encouraging me to leave. We walked arm-in-arm back to the car, where we sat for a few minutes in silence, watching the invisible air whip sand across the field. I took off my sandals and placed them in a bag, wanting to preserve them as though I was saving an artifact from an archaeological dig.

As we drove away from the cemetery, a haze closed over

the ghost town, and it faded into an ancient story before disappearing in the rearview mirror. For a few miles we let the silence roll out comfortably between us. I had come in search of a story that would not be unearthed and I was ready to surrender this loss, leave it in the cemetery beneath the rocks holding the sand against the wind. None of this could come with me. I could not make the unseeable materialize and my story, long invisible to me, would belong forever to the wild lands of West Texas. In the ghost town of Terlingua.

Chapter 14

REBRANDED

Cornwall, Pennsylvania: 2020

My mother passed away in May 2020, taking her story with her. Although she had been in ill health, suffering from dementia brought about by several strokes, at the age of 93, her death seemed untimely and shocking to me. She died in a nursing home in Texas during the pandemic lockdown, and, living more than two-thousand miles across the country, I could not get to her. She died alone–a fact that, to this day, haunts me. One night, three months after her death, I sat by myself in my living room and I began to cry, thinking about her, wondering if she had felt deserted at the end of her life. I must have fallen asleep, and it was the dream that woke me.

"I have a story, too," she said. "One that you'll have to tell for me."

Shaken by the sound of her voice, I got up and began to walk around my house, turning on all the lights on the first floor. I climbed to the second floor and continued to look for her. *Was I dreaming*? I walked up to the third floor, listening to every sound. It was late August and we kept the central air conditioner running twenty-four hours a day. I jumped when air began to flow through the vents. "Mom," I called out to her. "I'm here. Please talk to me." I stayed awake for several hours, waiting and hoping she'd speak to me again.

The next morning, while drinking coffee, I thought back to a visit I'd made four years before her death. Early in the summer of 2016, I flew from Pennsylvania to Texas to see her and, together, we drove from her apartment in San Angelo to her sister's house just outside Midland, some three hours away. A long drive on a flat highway across the desert. Several miles out of the city, ghostly wind turbines that now cover much of the terrain in Texas began to pop up across the horizon. Otherworldly and grand in scale, they resembled white apparitions gently moving air across the sky. Their arms waving us on, deeper into the desert. At first, they seemed to be nearby, but we drove ten more miles before reaching the base of the first group. Then more. Hundreds more wind turbines appeared as we drove.

The conversation was like so many others I'd had with her, the unspoken feeling of resentment present.

"You're getting too thin," she told me.

"Mom, please." I took a drink of my coffee and set it in the cup holder.

"I'm just saying this because I have a friend whose daughter died of anorexia," she added. *Could she be more dramatic?* I wasn't that thin.

"I'm only here for a few days. I'd like to enjoy our time together," I said.

Driving deeper into the desert, the horizon spread out with each mile, opening new vistas of red sand and cactus. A never-ending landscape. Two hours later, I turned the car down a red dusty lane and parked in front of my aunt's house. She lived in a large modular home, surrounded on all sides by a covered deck. I unloaded suitcases and carried them inside her house. We'd only planned to stay for a couple of days, but we had overpacked.

My aunt poured each of us a tall glass of iced tea and we retreated to the front porch, to relax in her old metal lawn chairs. Sitting in the shade, we watched heat mirages rising from the desert floor. I was always in awe of my aunt's composure. A fair-complected, auburn-haired petite woman, she sat serenely, listening deeply. *Always* listening deeply. She had a gift for perceiving what hadn't yet been said, her eyes flashing at some revelation she picked up from a casual comment. It was a quality that fascinated me. The heat and dryness got to be too much, and I wanted to go indoors where it was cool. Before I could suggest the idea, my mother broke in. Something about the setting must have triggered a memory for her.

"Do you remember all those years ago, when we sat in the shade, trying to stay cool by drinking orange Crush? It was the day of Mama and Daddy's wedding," she said.

I leaned forward in my chair and listened, anticipating a story I'd never heard. The sun glared, wind snapped, and red sand whipped a cloud across the yard, setting the stage for a drama, as my mother began to talk about the day of her parents' marriage.

"We were left in a car parked under a huge oak tree, just outside the Pecos County Courthouse, in Fort Stockton.

Remember?" The county, named for the river, was one of nine counties that made up the Trans-Pecos Region of West Texas, a powerful setting for a West Texas fable. "While we were left outside in the car, Mother and Daddy were married by the county judge," my mother explained.

Deanna rolled her eyes. "Oh, it was the big old gray Cadillac." She giggled.

I wondered if this could be the same lumbering car I'd seen in family photos but, before I could ask, they continued with the story.

My mother laughed. "Which time was that? You know, they were married at least twice."

The surprised look on my face didn't stop the sisters from talking. And giggling. I had heard several marriages mentioned in the past, but it was unusual for them to open up to me after carrying secrets for their entire lives. They sounded like little schoolgirls sharing clandestine tales for the first time.

My mother saw my confusion and added, "Oh, yes. They were married, then divorced, then re-married."

The sun began to move across the huge sky as they talked. Details about the old limestone courthouse, the intense heat, the oak tree. Their parents' divorce. I didn't ask questions for fear of stopping them from telling me the rest of the tale.

"We weren't scared, Glora." My aunt's West Texas pronunciation included dropping vowels from words. "We were happy with our soda."

They both rolled their eyes as they remembered their younger sister, Victoria, nicknamed Honey for her golden curls.

"She got fussy sitting in the backseat, so she climbed into the front of the car. Remember?"

I wondered how they remained calm, speaking matter-of-factly, as they revealed more about their parents' neglect. Apparently, leaving children alone in a car in the heat of the day was not unusual in West Texas.

My aunt got up and collected our empty glasses, carrying them inside on a wooden tray.

"Is there more to this, Mom? Is there anything…you know… more troubling that I should know about your childhood?" The look on my mother's face made it clear that I shouldn't ask more questions.

"Don't poke," she admonished me.

Deanna returned with freshly filled glasses of sweet tea. I looked up to see the sun had moved down across the horizon and begun to marbleize the sky pink and purple. Within a few minutes, it would yield itself to a velvety black veil punctuated by stars. I remembered folktales shared by workers in the industry, who used the phrase 'twinkling diamonds' to describe oil gushing from the land. An image that carried the promise of unexpected wealth for roustabouts and drillers who had staked their belongings and families to come to this arid desert in search of a new life. *Is that how my grandparents had felt on the day of their marriage? That they were re-inventing themselves and their lives?*

"Remember when Mother and Daddy moved us from Oklahoma to Texas, just before the wedding?" My aunt Deanna asked this time.

"Yes, we packed boxes, sealed them with tape, and Mother made us write the name 'France' on the outside of each one."

"What?" I asked. "Why France?"

My aunt chuckled and made a sound in her throat that sounded like a twangy guitar. "When we moved to Iraan, we weren't the France sisters any longer," she said. "After the move, Daddy adopted us and gave us his last name." Now I really needed to know more.

"Explain this to me. Your father adopted you?" I questioned.

I had known my mother was born in Shawnee, Oklahoma, in the winter of 1927, followed in two years by another sister and, seven years later, a second one. As the sisters continued to talk, the rest of the story began to come out. Their mother was a young single woman, involved in an affair with their father, who was married to a different woman at the time of their births. He had insisted the little girls be given a different surname so his would not be associated with them. My grandmother listed the name of Richard France on the birth certificates of each daughter. She agreed to cover up my grandfather's unfaithfulness to his wife.

What I didn't learn that late afternoon was just how many wives my grandfather had. I'd have guessed about three, maybe more. Apparently, he'd seen something in my grandmother—perhaps a need—that told him she would comply with his demands. While my grandfather remained with his previous wife until her death, the three little girls, known as the France Sisters, lived with their mother and maternal grandfather, "Ole Grand Dad." For several years, my grandmother supported her daughters, and, on occasions, like a winter squall, my grandfather blew into their home with gifts for everyone. His appearance was as unpredictable as the Oklahoma weather.

Listening to this account by the now-elderly sisters, I was able to trace the outline of an astonishing pattern of storytelling about disappearance and abandonment that had been imposed on their young lives. When their mother and father finally married, they were legally adopted — by their biological father — and the young France sisters became the Wilson girls. Overnight. My heart pounded, much like I imagined the land breaking open as an eruption of gushing oil tore apart the hard-panned dirt, throwing sand, rocks, and oil thousands of feet into the sky. This was part of West Texas ideology–the sudden explosion of new life, where dramatic change was an everyday event.

Years later, I decided to press my mother to explain to me why she had kept this secret. She said it was all about honor.

"Honoring who?" I asked.

"Well, she explained, "when my mother told us to do something, we listened and did just as she told us." One by one, my mother and her sisters had been given the surname of France and told to lie about their father, Samuel Wilson, to hide the truth about their identities.

Years later, I'd learn the man whose name was listed on their birth certificates, Richard France, was a stranger and had no biological connection to the sisters. At the time of birth, the identities of my mother and her sisters were altered on the records. Their original identities vanished.

On my mother's sixth birthday, after her biological father married her mother and officially gave his three little girls his last name, the new family moved out of the state of Oklahoma, deep into West Texas. In a town growing in wealth from the oil industry, my grandparents were able to create a new existence, a life that appeared to be comfortable on the surface. But they were never able to cover the pattern of disappearance, nor repair the harm of silencing three little girls. When I learned about this part of my mother's history, I understood how she lost her own voice. And I wondered how much of her soul had been stolen from her, left in Oklahoma.

I wondered if traces of her story remained in Shawnee, the town named for the Prairie Band Potawatomi Nation, a Native American tribe whose members were forcibly removed from their homelands under the federal government's Indian Removal Act. So many died during the march, it was named the Potawatomi Trail of Death. The Potawatomi Nation preserved their traditions, religions, and cultural history through storytelling, art, crafts, and music. I had to believe the land had absorbed these stories. It was against the backdrop of this history of forced removal where my mother and her sister's disappearance took place. I'd never been to Shawnee, but, in my heart, I was sure my mother's story lived on in the trees, the mountains, the sky. Just as the stories of the Potawatomi Nation had been witnessed and held by the rocks, the trees, the sky.

Knowing her history helped me understand her belief that it would not be harmful to remove me from my father's life. In her mind, asking a child to remain silent about abandonment was a not a form of neglect; rather, it was what reasonable people did with their children. All my life I had been angry at her for the disappearance of my sister and father, and I wanted to continue to blame her. But I couldn't.

As Adrienne Rich writes in her poem "Of Woman Born," "The woman I needed to call my mother was silenced before I was born." I suddenly knew that telling my own story depended on learning to tell my mother's and her mother's. More than my own silence was at stake, and it would demand a different kind of storytelling than I had practiced as a journalist, an academic, or a spiritual director.

Chapter 15

DECONSTRUCTED

Cornwall, Pennsylvania; Provence, France: 2022

In 2022, I was diagnosed with a bone disease. Osteoporosis. The diagnosis came after a bad year, in which I broke an arm, a toe, and a rib, all in minor home accidents. Before learning about my condition, I had made plans to travel with a group of 13 other women to the medieval town of Saint-Maximin-la-Sainte-Baume in Provence, France to see the basilica where the skull of Mary Magdalene is held in a gold reliquary. The pilgrimage would take us 1147 meters up the mountain of Sainte Baume, to reach the ancient sanctuary known as Mary Magdalene's grotto, carved by natural forces into a steep mountainous ledge in the French Alps. Called the Rock of Mercy, the site is one of the most famous religious destinations in the world. My tickets had been purchased and my bags were packed, but the story of my journey—what I called my *sacred bone journey*—began twenty-four hours before my flight, in my doctor's office.

I sat in the tiny examination room with my husband while a nurse took my vital signs and directed me to sit in the corner to wait for my primary care physician, a mature-age woman who resembled a wisdom keeper more than a physician. She had been great at offering down-home medical advice before prescribing chemicals to me.

"Let's start with the basics," she'd said when treating me in the past. I appreciated her directness and her refusal to mince words. She was running late this morning and, as I waited — for what seemed forever — I read the list of symptoms for COVID-19 and the CDC's guidelines for vaccinations. I combed through the literature on heart conditions. After about a half hour, she greeted us both, plopped down on her stool, and turned on the computer screen. She quickly pulled up the pictures of my bones, captured in a scan taken several weeks earlier.

Without explanation, she announced, "It's osteoporosis and it's bad. Don't fall. If you break your hip, you'll end up in a rehabilitation center." Suddenly, the plastic molded chair I was sitting on felt like iron.

"Good grief, that bad?" I took a deep breath, trying to absorb the diagnosis. "I'm going on a pilgrimage. I'm going to climb a huge mountain on ancient Roman roads," I told her. "My flight for France leaves tomorrow morning."

She squared her shoulders and looked straight into my eyes. Then, she pointed to the image on her computer screen. "This is serious. Look at the picture of your bones and the measurements. You can see how frail your hip bones are. I'm not saying you should miss the trip. I'm just advising you to be very careful."

Her earthy, round face did not smile, and the gravity in her voice concerned me. I had saved for a full year for this trip, taken classes on the history of Mary Magdalene, and read several books to prepare, including *The Gospel of Mary*. I would not be talked out of going. Nor would I let this diagnosis shape my experience.

This was the woman who had traveled with Jesus, who escaped persecution by coming to France. The woman who wrote her own Gospel, I thought. *She was the saint who risked her life to bring the story of the resurrection to Europe, who climbed the same mountain at my age. Hers was a much more dangerous journey than mine would be.*

I had been raised hearing about Jesus from white middle-aged ministers who quoted Paul, Peter, and Job, whose books fill the Bible. I wanted to know Jesus' story, told in the words of a woman whose experience in the world, though centuries earlier, was not unlike mine. I believed walking in the footsteps of this prophet, learning the secret lessons Jesus taught her, would deepen my spirituality.

Besides, even if her book had been written out of the canonical Bible, Mary Magdalene was the supreme story carrier. Her own story about a life dedicated to spreading Christianity across France was one I longed to know, to feel in my bones. I had to follow her. To walk the path followed by popes, kings, crusaders, and pilgrims all in search of her spiritual presence. I promised my physician I'd be careful. The next morning, my husband and friends drove me to Philadelphia where I boarded the plane for a long flight to Marseilles, France.

The trip could not have been more miserable. Extra transfers, packed airports, a shortage of staff, tough security requirements, and seats with no leg room. I carried a pair of hiking sticks with me on the plane, through the airport, and through long lines in customs and security. I wore a backpack, which slowed me down. The flight, including layovers, was about eighteen hours long. When I finally arrived in France, my feet and legs were swollen, my baggage was lost and, with it, all my vitamins and prescriptions to treat osteoporosis. I searched the baggage claim area, spoke with the airlines, all to no avail. My belongings were gone.

Determined, I was not about to let this interrupt my mission, so I caught the airport shuttle to the nearby Holiday Inn, checked into a room, and met up with my travel companion, Mary, a scholar of the Black Madonnas and a seeker of the Magdalene tradition. The next morning, we gathered with the members of the pilgrimage group and boarded a van for the long drive to the town of St. Maximin-la-Sainte-Baume.

Within a day of arriving, I began to feel the stress in my body. My bones and joints ached. My doctor had warned me not to do yoga, not even to stretch or bend over at the waist. "No twisting your spine," she had said. "You could break a tiny bone." Still, I had come to walk up the mountain and I was not about to change my plans. On day three of the journey, we assembled at the base of St. Baume to get instructions from the pilgrimage leader, a lecturer and resident of the area whose family had been involved with leading local ceremonies and festivities honoring Mary Magdalene for over 700 years.

"Stay together and move slowly up the path," she told us. That's when I realized, in my rush to get out of the hotel that morning, I forgot to bring my walking sticks and I was wearing my hot pink Nikes, which were more useful for short walks than long mountain pilgrimages. We entered the ancient forest leading to the mountain path, named for the mythical goddess Artemis, and, just as I expected, the old Roman roads had been washed out by heavy rains. I slipped and slid on large rocks and pebbles as we climbed. The leader kept a close watch on us to make sure we were all safe. When I found a large tree branch on the ground, I picked it up and used it to balance myself. And I stopped every so often to rest.

In the back of my mind was my doctor's warning, "Don't fall. Don't break a bone." Nothing would discourage me. I was on the hunt—following Mary's legend. I was in search of the story of the woman who I saw as a prophet, an activist who, by carrying the tale of the Resurrection across the sea, evangelized Europe.

The air in the forest was heavy with dampness, yet sparking with excitement, an energy held in place by old growth deciduous trees, beech, lime, ash, elm, and maple, as well as woodland growth unique to the forest. Cutting trees was forbidden in the sacred forest. After all, these trees had stood as witnesses to Mary's ascent, as well as the passage of hundreds of saints and pilgrims who followed her. They were present on the mountain when it was known as "our mother of the waters," when druids practiced rites on the site. I moved carefully, stepping slowly, and stopping to study shrines built along the path. The vibrational quality in the forest seemed to deepen with each step. I pushed on, climbing the steep path up to the pinnacle. The last few hundred feet consisted of vertical, narrow stone steps, with an old handrail on one side.

After more than an hour of climbing, I reached the plaza outside the grotto on the side of the mountain, with my travel companions. We gathered in front of a large stone wall at the bronze statue of the Virgin Mary holding her son Jesus in his death. Mary Magdalene was at his feet. I was overcome by the power of the piece, and stood before it quietly, for several minutes. Then, I moved close to the rock ledge and leaned over to get a look at the sheer drop of the bluish-colored cliff to the expansive valley of Provence below. Turning to look from a different angle felt like looking through a new lens. I turned to the right, then to the left, getting a new view each time, as though I were looking through a spiritual kaleidoscope that changed the makeup of the world beneath. Seeing what could not be seen from the ground below. I was out of breath, overcome with pain, exhaustion, and awe, but humbled to be in this sacred location.

I sat outside on the cool stone bench with my sister travelers for a few minutes. Eileen, from Ireland, cried gently. The sparkle in Brandie's dark eyes was matched by her beautiful smile. We were all taken by the beauty, by the supernatural feel, and by the silence that held centuries of legend and history.

After a few minutes, I began to climb the steep, almost vertical steps leading to the sanctuary, known as Mary Magdalene's cave. Standing at the entry, I paused to feel the mystical essence that touched my skin before crossing the threshold that separated the outer world from the space where saints and goddesses had entered to worship. It was damp and dark, and I sought the only available light source, a series of stained-glass windows above the entry. After my eyes adjusted, I walked very carefully across the damp floor and descended the steep stone steps to the darkest part of the cave where Mary's statue was placed in a candlelit corner.

The darkness obscured several puddles of water and when I stepped into one, I thought, *Water. Sacred water. Mary had also come across the sea, from Palestine, and she was led to this cavern carved on the side of a mountain by water. She had descended into the dark, moist womb of the mountain where the divine feminine essence was present. I was here, too, absorbing the same moisture into the cells of my body. Standing in the same silence. In the same stillness, where Mary had brought Jesus' message about turning inward to feel loved.*

There was no handrail to help me climb back up the steps, so I moved carefully on the old narrow treads. But the challenge was not over. I still had to get down the mountain and knew the descent would be more difficult than the climb to the top. Fortunately, two of the women on the pilgrimage saw me struggling to maintain my balance on the loose stones and held me by the arms as we inched back down the steep path. This, to me, was the essence of sisterhood, the gift of *anam cara*, sacred friendship.

By the time we arrived at the hotel that evening, I could barely move. The ache in my body was bone deep: my back, my hips, my legs. I picked up my cell phone and called the pilgrimage leader, Veronique, who was also a health practitioner. "I can't go with the group tomorrow," I told her. "I'm in too much pain."

"I want to help you," Veronique offered. I knew she grew flowers and herbs at her home and mixed them into oils. Over dinner the previous night, she had explained how she came by the recipes for mixing the oils. "These are found in the Bible. The ancients used oils to heal, bring joy, to honor."

"I would appreciate any help, Roni," I told her. I hung up the phone, took two Tylenol, and went to bed.

The next morning, I was roused from sleep by a loud pounding on my hotel room door. It was Veronique, carrying a bottle of oil she had prepared for me. "This," she said, "will reduce the swelling and...here," she reached inside the door, "is a bottle of pills for the pain." I thanked her, rubbed the oil all over my body, took the pills, and fell into a deep sleep, dreaming about Mary and her travel companions sailing across the sea on the crashing waves. It had been a treacherous and, admittedly, somewhat dangerous trip for me to make with this medical condition; but it was a journey of solidarity, one sister with another, across the centuries, a tribute to the woman whose life was dedicated to carrying the ultimate tale of all time. I was groggy but in much less pain. The rest of the pilgrimage group had gone on without me, to visit another sacred site, so I remained in bed for the afternoon.

I knew my body was trying to speak to me through the pain, to give me a message; it had been carrying stories in my bones. I felt the call into what Jungian analyst Marion Woodman describes as goddess energy, "the unspeakable wisdom that grows in the very cells of the body...the beauty and the horror of the whole of life." I knew the other women on the pilgrimage all had been infused with the same power. Now, they also would carry it in their bodies. That evening I re-joined the group for dinner. We sat around a long, linen-covered table in a dining room separated from other hotel guests. The room was dark, lit only by large candles set in the middle of the table.

When there was a lull in the conversation, I spoke, expressing my belief that, "Mary Magdalene had carried the story of Jesus up this mountain. Now, we are all carrying Mary Magdalene's story in our bones."

In my mind, we were now the bearers of a sacred tale that had burrowed itself deep in our marrow, a story so powerful it would persist for many more centuries, carried by pilgrims. Several days later, on my flight back home to Pennsylvania, I thought about Mary's mission, wondering if she had fully realized the magnitude of the story she carried. A story that would change the history of the world. Then I wondered if, like Mary, I was also carrying a tale about my family, bigger than I could imagine. One made more powerful by its inaccessibility.

Chapter 16

RECOVERED

Cornwall, Pennsylvania: 2020

I never met my great-grandmother Vina, never even saw her photo. Her name was never mentioned in my family. What little I knew about her came from my grandmother, Mommy, who told us that her mother and father, Vina and Jesse, abandoned her at the age of six, taking her to live on her grandparents' ranch in West Texas. We never knew the entire story, and no one really pursued it until more than eighty-five years after her death when we found Vina buried on the grounds of the San Antonio State Hospital where she lived the last fifteen years of her life. In an asylum.

When I ran across her, I didn't know what to think about Vina. She seemed to be an unusual aside, an interesting character, but not one that could offer me any insight into my family's story. Plus, she had never really been part of my life. I put aside her information for years, until, returning from my pilgrimage to southern France, I suddenly felt a strong desire to reach deeper into the history of my ancestors. The mystical experience in Mary Magdalene's cave had triggered a curiosity about ancient stories that were held in dark, deep places, remaining hidden for centuries. Had Mary Magdalene been pointing me toward a crucial event in my family? Perhaps, toward Vina?

As I searched, I found several accounts of Vina's story, each one more mysterious than the other. Her life did not reveal itself all at once; rather, the tale unfolded in bits and pieces of confusing information. One version had it that she was married in 1906 and her daughter, Wilhemena (Mommy), was born the next year. Three years later, she divorced her husband, or he divorced her. The exact order isn't known. Mother and daughter moved in with Vina's parents, William and Frances McLanahan. Then, for some reason, in 1915, Vina was admitted to the San Antonio State Hospital. She was released four years later in "improved condition," and re-admitted again in 1919, followed by a final commitment in 1921. She died in the asylum in 1935, from tuberculosis.

I wondered if Vina had been committed with a mental health diagnosis or, as so many TB sufferers were at that time, institutionalized. I went immediately to an academic medical site to read up on psychiatric diagnoses for women in the early 20th century. At that time, it was not uncommon for psychiatrists to commit women who deviated from the "naturally submissive role of wife and mother."

I wondered if Vina had been a victim of the prevailing medical wisdom that demonized women who spoke out, expressed ambition, and declined to follow the direction of their husbands. I cringed. In that climate, it would have been easy for a husband to commit his wife. According to the research, women were generally put away without evidence of mental deficiency. Kate Moore's Time Magazine article, titled "Declared Insane by Speaking Up: The American History of Silencing Women Through Psychiatry," described this as an extreme practice [that] mirrored existing misogynistic beliefs about women and sexuality of the time. For weeks, I sought more information but, despite my efforts, there seemed to be nothing to explain her hospitalization. I wanted to ask someone in my family: my grandmother, my mother. But they were gone.

The idea that my great-grandmother had been held in an asylum for much of her adult life troubled me, reviving memories of my own difficult childhood, as well as stories about women across the ages, such as Mary Magdalene, who were maligned and made to vanish. As disconcerting as this information was, I would discover more details about Vina's life in the next few years. Facts that were even more disturbing than an archaic psychiatric diagnosis.

Two years after finding Vina's death certificate, I sat in my office pouring over the 1930 census. It was a sunny afternoon and light filled the room. Tina Turner's meditative chant, "Mother Within," played in the background, her voice awakening a sadness in me that had been present in my childhood. I read on, until my eyes focused on a line where Vina was listed as an "inmate," living in the San Antonio area. I looked at the word again. "Inmate." *Why hadn't she been listed as a patient?* The term felt inhumane. I wasn't sure I could trust what I was reading — the characterization of her in this way seemed to silence her, dismiss her, make her invisible.

Tina's voice echoed in the room, causing me to sigh as she chanted about being lost and alone.

I read further to another entry. "Patient in custody of her father." I did a quick search and discovered an old newspaper article reporting a time when the state asylum had become overcrowded, and patients were discharged early. Some were moved to the local jails. *Had she been one of them? Was that the reason she was listed as an inmate on the census?*

An Indian songstress broke into Tina's chant, with a line in Sanskrit that sounded like a primeval call. I wondered what else I would find.

What had happened to Vina? I wondered. *What happened to her child during those years?* I was alarmed at the idea that Mommy, who was told she was abandoned by her parents, was actually the child of a woman who had been left in a state institution. Mother and daughter had suffered the same assault on their souls. The very idea gave me chills and I sat, holding documents, hoping for guidance, even a clue that could clear up the mystery. One thing was undeniable. Vina's story — which had never been shared with anyone in my family — had not disappeared with her death. It had endured in the form of a family legacy, a tale that returned as an emotional inheritance, traveling from one generation of women to the next. I thought about the horror Vina must have felt. I became overwhelmed and went outside to sit in the sunshine.

For weeks, I was unsettled by the idea that my grandmother, Mommy, had never been told about her mother's hospitalization, nor about her death. It broke my heart, too, to think that my great-grandmother, my grandmother, and my mother all would have been alive at the same time, but never known of the others' existence. Months later, I decided to try again to find the rest of the story–or, at least, some additional pieces.

I went back over old conversations I'd had with my mother while she was still alive. Perhaps I had missed something. I thought back to a phone conversation we'd had two years before her death when my mother's mind was still clear.

"Tell me all you remember," I begged her.

"All I ever knew, is that Vina's mother and father just dropped her off at Ole Grandad's ranch."

I pressed her for more information. "Why?"

"I never was told why they did it." She seemed to be telling me the truth.

I asked if Mommy had ever seen her parents again.

"Well, I heard that once in a while a man would show up at the ranch, saying he was an uncle," my mother offered.

"Was he? An uncle?" Surely, I thought, my mother would remember something about the situation.

"I don't know. He sometimes brought a toy, a doll, but he never stayed very long."

I could hear my mother's voice growing thick and decided to stop grilling her. She really did not know. I wanted to cry, too. For my grandmothers, my mother, and for myself.

"It must have been shattering for the little girl who was isolated, on a West Texas ranch with elderly grandparents," I said, drawing the phone call to an end. We both knew we weren't any closer to understanding the story.

Over the next year, my search looked like an amateur seamstress' effort to attach pieces of fabric with a slender thread that dissolved with one twist, leaving me carrying a heavy rope of guilt. *My God,* I thought, *I am a researcher. I should be able to do this.* I knew we were all carrying Vina's story, whatever the story was. I was tempted to give up and accept the cryptic details I did have.

One evening, after a long day of phone calls, talking to county officials about birth and death records, I fell asleep and dreamt about Vina. In my dream, the bedroom was shrouded in blackness, like heavy drapes. I thought I heard a voice and sat up in bed. My night-light, which usually illuminated the floor, was not working, but I heard a faint noise as the door opened. I looked up to see a woman standing there. She wasn't exactly solid — more like a silhouette. I stared at her for a minute until my vision cleared and I could see her face. Encircled in a haze of gray clouds, she stood in the doorway, almost as though she was too frightened to enter the room. Then, she placed one foot inside and stood with the other still in the hallway.

"I'm Vina," she said. She was small, her voice like that of a child. Her pale face was drawn tight, save for delicate wrinkles around her mouth and eyes. *Those eyes — hypnotic, what my mother would call "gypsy eyes."* Her thin white-gray hair barely covered her head. The single rose she held in her hand filled the room with a soft scent.

"Vina?" I gasped. "My great-grandmother?" Her eyes flashed in the night like sparkling jewels, and she looked directly at me. Behind her, a backdrop began to come into focus — it was a pale blue sky that faded into the edges of the darkened walls of the bedroom. Cracked earth stretched out beneath her feet, seeming to reach back years into her youth. A large, multi-story old white building with a red roof was behind her. It was the asylum, just as it had appeared in the photo of the state hospital posted on the website. The symbol of her incarceration.

But here she was. Vina was free. She had escaped the grave and come into my dream.

I didn't know what to say. I wanted to ask her about the chaos in her life. I reached across the bed, toward her, but she faded into the mist. She was gone. I pushed off the blankets and began to get up and walk toward the door. So many people had vanished from my life. I wondered where she had gone. Had she returned to the grave? To the same patient cemetery on the grounds of the hospital?

Now fully awake, I sat down on the bed, looked over to see my husband sleeping, and decided not to wake him. Sitting in the pitch-black room for a while, I wondered if I had dreamt about Vina or been visited by her ghost. Or had she been an apparition? Finally, just before falling asleep again, a bit of insight came to me. A whispering in my heart that brought the vision of Vina into focus. Just as I had been abandoned, just as my mother and her mother had been deserted, Vina had, herself, been forsaken. By her husband. By her father. By her family, who seemed to know nothing about her. *Here it was*, I thought. *Vina brought the story I carried. We all carried.* It had traveled across generations to appear at the foot of my bed. The truth was hard to hold. *But it was the real story. It was, right?*

When I awoke the next morning, my heart was heavy, as I

recalled the little woman in my bedroom. I wished I'd had the presence of mind to ask Vina more questions. She must have wondered why no one had ever come to rescue her. I regretted not expressing my sorrow that she died alone.

Aloud, I said to myself, "If she had come to me in the middle of the night, it might have been to share something with me." Pulling myself back into reality, I answered, "But this was my story, right? I was the child who had been abandoned by a father and sister and removed by a mother, taken in the night."

Did Vina know my story? My mind seemed to be so fuzzy, like a spider's sticky web, and I couldn't seem to make the dream make sense. I got out of bed, pulled the clean white sheets tight across the mattress, and gently covered them with the comforter. I fluffed each pillow cover and carefully arranged pale sky-blue accent pillows on the bed, just beneath the painting of white orchids. I studied the flowers in the painting closely — were there fourteen this morning, instead of thirteen? Slowly, the world began to feel right again, orderly. Organized. Clean.

I went outside to inspect the flowers in my garden. Heavy gray clouds filled the sky, but my sunflowers seemed poised to bloom, cosmos winked with delicacy, and zinnias stood straight against the white fence. Were there more dahlias blooming in the pots on the front porch this morning? Or had they been there yesterday, showing off their delicate petals and mauve color?

I removed my shoes and stood on the enriched garden soil, allowing the night's rain to soak into my skin. I checked the rocks that lined the flower and tiny vegetable gardens, straightening those I found out of place. With each task, I was putting things back into order, trying to replace the scene I had witnessed in my bedroom the previous night. Standing in the daylight, I told myself that Vina's life was not my life. Her story was not my story. *It had been a dream.* Still, all day long, I looked over my shoulder as I moved from room to room. No one was there, but I felt Vina's presence.

Two years later in 2022, I discovered yet another piece of Vina's story, and it was bigger than any myth, legend, or dream. Out of the blue, new information came to me, revealing that she had been the victim of something even more sinister than I could have imagined. In March, my husband and I flew to San Antonio to visit my brother and his wife, along with other family members and friends. Several days into the visit, we rented a car and drove 270 miles to the Rio Grande Valley, where we met up with two friends from the Mary Magdalene pilgrimage.

We had made plans to see the Black Madonna at the Basilica of the National Shrine of Our Lady San Juan Del Valle. Five months earlier, in France, I'd first experienced the power of the Black Madonna and been taken immediately by her mysterious essence, her Blackness, and the stories of miracles that surrounded her. On returning home from the Magdalene pilgrimage, I'd convinced my husband to go with me to Doylestown, Pennsylvania to the National Shrine of Our Lady of Czestochowa, the American shrine honoring the famous Black Madonna in Czestochowa, Poland. This Black Madonna had been declared the queen and protector of Poland after saving the monastery at Jasna Gora from a Swedish invasion. It was only an hour away from our house and I needed to again be in the presence of the Madonna. I was in awe of the lore and legend around these icons to the divine feminine, but I still could not get a grasp on my own fascination with her, the reason I felt a personal connection to her.

The history of miracles associated with the thousands of Black Madonnas around the world drew most seekers to them, but there was something else that spoke to me. While in France, I'd learned that some of the icons had been buried, kept underground for centuries, hidden and kept from harm during enemy attacks until they could be safely unearthed in Europe, Africa, and America. Perhaps, something about being shrouded in darkness and hidden tapped into an untold story hidden in my soul. I sensed that visiting a Black Madonna in South Texas — where my family's story had been obscured would help me exhume pieces of my own history. Fragments of stories about my family that had been buried with my great-grandmother.

We left early in the morning, hoping to miss heavy traffic and drove in rain for most of the trip. As we neared the border, the sky grew dark and opened up, inundating the expansive valley in a downpour. The weather turned chilly, so when we arrived, we went straight to the basilica and checked into the hotel owned by the church. My friends arrived an hour later, and, together, we walked the short distance to the basilica. It was a stunning building, filled with other pilgrims seeking the miracles offered by Our Lady San Juan Del Valle. Some had come seeking healing from injuries and illnesses. We walked silently in and out of candlelit rooms filled with religious icons, statues, and artwork — including a stunning painting of Mary

Magdalene. Then we broke apart and went through the church on our own.

Alone, I walked to the front of the sanctuary, behind the altar and down to the lower level where the statue of the Black Madonna of San Juan Del Valle filled the entire wall. She was grand. Circled by golden rays, twelve stars, and carvings of indigenous folk who lived in the valley, alongside missionaries from the church. She seemed to preside over the area from on high. The room was filled with hundreds of fresh flowers, mostly roses. Several people knelt at the foot of the statue to light candles and pray. I found a bench out of the way and sat, silently asking the Madonna for help to write the story that would bring some healing to my family. After a few minutes, I walked back into the sanctuary, and took a seat with my husband and friends. We stayed for the bilingual mass, then went to a local Mexican restaurant for dinner. The entire experience had felt magical. But, as we drove back to the hotel in the dark, I wasn't sure anything would come of it.

That night, storms kept me awake, as thunder rolled across the valley and lightning seemed to strike close outside our window. It poured for hours, and I couldn't get warm. We both awoke early, feeling chilled, and I wanted to get dressed and get on the road to drive back to San Antonio. After breakfast, we said goodbye to our friends and began the long return trip. I had mixed feelings about leaving my friends so early, but something was pulling me back up north. A voice deep within me said, "Come, now." Several hours later, as we neared the city, the sun broke out across the big Texas sky, making it uncomfortably warm. I leaned forward to turn up the air conditioning and suddenly felt a bolt of energy run through me—a strong desire to reach out to Vina.

I looked at my husband and said, "Let's see if we can visit her grave at the state hospital." We weren't far from the old asylum where she was buried.

"What?" my husband said, surprised. "We're hitting a lot of traffic now. Maybe we should have planned this earlier."

I hadn't thought about a visit until just this moment, but my longing to connect with my great-grandmother was strong, and rather than respond to him, I looked up the hospital and dialed the number. It took several tries to get the information. The woman in the records office told me Vina was listed under her father's last name, rather than her married name. When she asked me for Vina's date of death, I had to leave the call to search for it online and call her again. "April 5, 1935," I told her. Traffic was getting heavy, so my husband pulled the car over at an exit. Finally, the woman helping me was able to locate Vina's hospital records but told me a visit could not be arranged for another week. I protested. "Next week?"

"Hundreds of patients were buried here, ma'am," she explained. "We'd have to reach the groundskeeper and have him locate the grave. That takes time."

We were scheduled to fly home to Pennsylvania in two days, so a visit would not be possible. Larry reached over and held my hand. "I know you're disappointed. I'm sorry," he said.

I had been so close to finding Vina or finding out more about her and I had to do *something*. I couldn't leave the state without knowing more. Although I had just seen it, I returned a second time to the family ancestry file to verify Vina's date of death.

"April 5, 1935. That's only four days from now," I announced. "Could she be reaching out to me? Again?"

On a whim, I called the hospital once more; this time, to ask about the possibility of securing her medical records. The same woman in the records office answered and immediately put me on hold. After waiting for several minutes, she returned, telling me to submit a formal request, with a copy of my driver's license. She told me how to locate the request form online and submit it. "That's all I have to do," I told my husband. "I can't believe it. Now maybe I'll finally get some idea about what happened to Vina."

Two days later when we got home, I wrote to hospital officials and a response came within forty-eight hours. I printed out the pages, eight in all. They were copies of microfiche file pages, dark, shadowy pieces, and very hard to read. I grabbed my glasses and ran downstairs to share them with Larry.

"Look what I've got," I exclaimed. He was making coffee for the next morning and the smell of French roast filled the room. "Hurry." I sat down at the table, spreading out the sheets, and asked him to look over the papers with me. "I can't believe they actually released these to me." I held the pages up and tried to read the entries about Vina's admission, the dates, her diagnoses, all handwritten in a light-colored, ghostly-looking ink. It was hard to make out entire sentences. Suddenly, about five pages into the packet, I came across her evaluation. The statement stuck out like neon lighting on the black page, explaining that she had been committed to the hospital by court order, while serving a jail sentence for "shooting her father." I screamed, "Shooting her father? What the hell!!"

Larry grabbed for the papers. "Let me see this." He got a magnifying glass out of the kitchen junk drawer and looked over the page. "It says she was taken to the hospital from jail after shooting her father." We looked at each other in disbelief. I dropped the page and sat back in the chair, trying to let the information sink in.

"Shot him?" I had to say it aloud. Again and again, I repeated, "She shot her father." I stood up and walked across the open room, trying to absorb what I had just read. I fixed my eyes on the trees outside my house, hoping that one of the deer that frequently visited my back yard would appear now. I needed some kind of sign. "You mean Vina, my great-grandmother, who was in her late twenties and had a child, picked up a gun, aimed it at her father and shot him?" My husband looked at me, shook his head, and resumed his reading of the pages to himself.

From across the room, I yelled, "There is more to this story. Why would a young woman do such a thing?!" This made no sense. I wanted to know why she had resorted to violence. *What would make her want to attack her father? Why would any woman use violence? Unless....unless he had done something so terrible that she couldn't imagine any other way to respond. But, shooting him? Had he hurt her?* I realized, Vina's child, my grandmother, Mommy, was just a little girl at the time. *Had she seen any of this? Had she been hurt? She must have been traumatized.* My mind was racing, and I didn't know what upset me more: the shooting, Mommy's safety, or Vina's incarceration and commitment.

It was devastating to read the rest of the details about Vina.

146

"Total overall time in the hospital: 17 years." I began to cry. "My God. She was alone. She was abandoned…to die."

For days, I ran over the story in my mind, trying to make it feel real. Or make the words feel less awful. I had no one to turn to for clarification. I knew Vina's father had survived the shooting and he and his wife took Mommy away to live with them. I suddenly realized my skepticism of the stories I'd heard about Mommy's childhood had been dead right. I had always questioned the family's story. Now, I knew the original tale was not true. She had not been abandoned by her mother. She had been taken.

Later in the week as we sat over dinner, I said to my husband, "It's all beginning to come together. The hidden story." We talked about the shooting, and I became more distressed over questions that could not be answered. Vina's child was taken away by the man she shot, and he became her legal guardian, raising the little girl with his wife. He must have lied to hide the truth. Then, many years later, after his wife died and he became elderly, Mommy, who was then an adult with her own children, took him in to live with her and her three little girls. This was the man who told his granddaughter, Mommy, that her mother had abandoned her. This was the man my mother and her sisters called 'Ole Grandad.'

I thought of the handwritten entries that had been so hard to see on the pages of the dark microfiche hospital files; they held the horrific truth. I'd never know the reason for the shooting, but the very idea that this man, "Ole Grandad," had been living in the house with these little girls, one of them my own mother, was unsettling. At the time, Mommy was raising her daughters alone because the man who was their biological father was married to another woman and he did not acknowledge them as his daughters. He forced Mommy to hide them away, by listing another man's name on their birth certificates, until, following the death of his wife, he married her and adopted the three little girls. His daughters. I never knew what happened to "Ole Grandad." I didn't know when he died, nor where he was buried.

Eventually, I began to string together pieces of all the stories and a pattern took shape out of the mess. It was an outline for the story of my own disappearance. By the time I was born, three generations of women in my family had been abandoned and the model had traveled so deep, so far, it no longer seemed unusual. Each one of us–my great-grandmother, my grandmother, my mother, and I–had been removed, hidden. All of us.

The women in my family, indeed, had lived lives of mythic proportions, not unlike the goddesses on Mt. Olympus. We could no more protect ourselves from being disappeared than could the goddess Persephone, who was abducted and taken to the dark underworld by Hades. The power of the connection hit me: disappearance, banishment. It was an ancient story that linked the women in my family to the fate of so many women. Disturbing? Yes. Some might describe it as a tale of women who were living out a legacy of intergenerational trauma, doomed to repeat tragic experiences. But over the months as the details began to settle into all the areas of my mind and my soul, I started to see things differently.

We would not be contained in a box that labeled us as broken women and hidden away. Our stories were bigger, more significant. Not unlike the Black Madonnas that had been hidden underground around the world for centuries, and were eventually discovered, the women in my family were also coming out of the darkness. Our lives were being unearthed. And we were emerging as a tribe of story carriers with untold tales, passed from one female ancestor to the next. I belonged to this tribe. Now I had to honor the women in my family, including those not yet born, by telling the real story. I had to free Vina from the silence that had kept her hidden for so many years. I had to free all of us by recovering the story.

Chapter 17

RETURNED

West Texas: 2021

For years after being taken away from my childhood home in West Texas, I'd returned to visit the little town: to see the library in the center of town, organized by my grandmother; the old school where I'd attended kindergarten for several weeks before we moved to Europe; the house where I'd stayed with my grandmother as a tiny child; the old Methodist Church. The long drive across the desert had always felt like a mystical experience, a trip that took me back to an archaic place in my life. In 1986, I drove toward the town, pointing my small car down Highway 190 into the Pecos Valley, counting the miles and plateaus, and listening to the radio.

Just as I crested the hill, where the sallow sand became pinkish-red, Don Henley's voice rang out, singing "Hotel California," and it sounded like he was describing the scenery ahead of me. The terrain opened to reveal an immense sky, and I felt myself drifting into a dizzying other-worldly place in my heart. I felt the return of a familiar mixture of excitement about the possibility of finding someone who knew my story, and dread brought on by the memory of my early childhood.

Thirty-five years later, in the summer of 2021, I returned again with my brother Joseph and my husband, carrying my mother's remains a year after her death. The COVID-19 lockdown had delayed travel for over a year and, as soon as the country opened up, we flew from Pennsylvania to Texas where my brother drove us west to perform the family ritual. Sitting in the backseat of my brother's red SUV, I held the wooden box of her ashes, as he drove down the highway toward her childhood home just outside Iraan. We were not exactly sure of the spot to turn into the old homestead, but when my stomach began to churn and the feeling of dread hit me, I said, "We must be close." At the bend in the highway, the sky spread out before us, the plateau giving way to the desert below and miles of flat land.

"This is it," Joe said, turning the car onto a dusty road. A few hundred feet farther down the rocky path, he stopped the car in the middle of the lane. We got out and walked across an open field, searching for signs of the old ranch. Immediately, I was hit with a gust of dry, dusty wind and thought, *There it is. The wind I've always detested.* Steadying myself, I turned to face the sun as if to challenge it. We walked on just a bit farther, through desert scrub and sticker-covered ground before spotting the rocks. *The foundation of the old ranch.*

"I feel comfortable that this is the right spot," my brother said. We gathered around the rocks, standing silently for a few moments. Then Joseph took the box from me, opened it, and grabbed a handful of dust, saying, "We got as close as we could to your old home, Mom." I watched the delicate white flakes disappear into the sky. It was my turn. I reached in, filling my hand with her remains and released her.

"We love you, Mother." When I spoke, the wind stopped blowing and the world felt very different to me, less threatening. "I need to remember this experience," I whispered to myself.

We walked quietly back to the car, got in, and backed out of the lane. I thought, *It is this simple, to disappear someone. To release a loved one.*

We had one more stop to make on our desert pilgrimage, so my brother aimed the car back onto the highway, turning down the hill to the entrance of Resthaven, the little cemetery located near the Pecos River, just outside Iraan. We'd decided to do a final scattering of my mother's ashes on my grandmother's grave. Watching the hill recede behind us, I was overcome with a longing in my heart, mixed with sadness about the place I had once hated: the desert, complicit in my childhood disappearance, and the sky that had witnessed my young life. Unsure if the land even remembered me, I thought, *What did I want? It was a desolate landscape, incapable of holding onto anything in this heat and wind.* Maybe I needed to believe the sand, the rocks, the sky felt some responsibility for knowing my family's stories. "Surely, the sun had recognized me," I told myself, When we arrived at the cemetery, we found the entrance closed—highway crews had just deposited black tar on the road, and we couldn't drive over it to reach my grandmother's grave. All I could say was, "This desert highway is leading us to hell."

Joe parked the car outside the gate, along the shoulder of the highway, and we began walking directly across the black road, just far enough to get to the grass. We'd come too many miles not to finish our mission. The rubber soles on my sandals stuck to the tar, so I tried to tiptoe across the road. On the other side, the grass was dead; all that remained was sand and patches of scrub. *This is hell,* I thought.

Each step triggered a memory of my grandmother, my mother, my sister, my father, the home we lost. *I've got to keep walking until we find her grave.* Suddenly, I saw it. A thin, black form, about a hundred feet away. As we got closer, the form took shape and I could see it was the same wrought iron shepherd's hook my brother and I had buried in the ground above my grandmother's grave on the day of her funeral, sixteen years ago. The one with wind chimes that clashed in the sunshine and wind, seeming to sing to me of her presence. The pole was leaning over toward the ground a bit and, when we got closer, I could see that only a piece of the filament string was still hanging from the top. The glass chimes were gone, probably broken in the winds.

"Do you believe this?" I said. "It's still here, after all this time." It seemed implausible to me that the hook survived in this open, dry terrain, in a cemetery that had hardly been maintained. Under my breath, I whispered, "The wind chimes on the hook — they caught her stories, the ones we shared about my grandmother at her burial." Stories about her as a horsewoman, a rancher's wife, beloved teacher, and historian. We stood over Mommy's grave for just a few moments, hoping to scatter the final bit of my mother's ashes before the wind picked up. We split the remains left in the bag and holding them in my hand, I was surprised to hear myself saying, "Now, Mother, your stories will blow in the wind, to join your daughter's, your mother's, and her mother's stories." I knew I was not speaking only to myself, nor to my husband or brother. Someone else was listening, someone who, like the wind, could not be seen. A felt presence.

I turned to look around but no one else was there. Still, something was calling me, and I realized it was the wind, asking me to open up my soul enough to allow a story to blow inside. I stood still with this idea for a few minutes as the wind picked up again, gently blowing against my skin, through my hair. For the first time, I felt like one with the land on which I stood. The wind was alive, moving my family's stories across the horizon into a time I could not see–*Kairos*, or sacred time. It was carrying me across a threshold where I could feel the presence of those who had disappeared from my life. We were all connected by the rhythm of the story's heartbeat. I stood firm, like an ancient tree, allowing the wind to touch me, no longer feeling unsafe in the world.

That night, I recalled the dream I'd had about six months after my mother's death, in which she seemed to give me her blessing. In my dream, we stood in my flower garden, surrounded by orange and deep sienna ruffled marigolds.

"Mother," I said. "Please forgive me for telling this story."

She smiled at me and, without speaking, bent over to pick one of the flowers. She held the bud in her hands, crushing it until the seeds were visible. She reached toward me, dropping the tiny black kernels into my heart. Then she vanished without saying a word. I knew the dream had carried a message to me about the nature of disappearance and appearance. As I thought about it over the next few days, I began to understand that my early losses were like the marigold seeds I'd planted in the late spring, which pushed through the darkness and blossomed in the sun. At the end of the season as the flowers withered, the petals opened to release seeds held in the plant's pod. Now, as a story carrier facing the end of the season, I was ready to share my stories with a new generation of women in my family. To bring back the tales that had disappeared.

Epilogue:

RE-IMAGED

Cornwall, Pennsylvania: 2023

One cool morning in mid-May, I sat at my writing desk on the third floor of my house, watching the season change outside the window. This was the forest's annual translucent-green light show, pushing fleshy leaves through the bony fingers of new limbs, trailing off thick branches of the trees. Maples, oaks, hickory, mountain laurel, some entwined by wild honeysuckle vines. Three weeks ago, the green of buds shone through the limbs; then, without notice, they exploded. All on a schedule beyond my understanding. This year, a few trees remained bare, their trunks a pale grayish-brown. Soon, it would be the time of the year when one or two heavy spring rainstorms would cause a tree to release its footings and fall to the ground. Turning away from the scene, I looked back at the open document on the computer screen, trying once more to write the final chapter of my story, which had felt incomplete, elusive. *Why couldn't I find the end of the story?*

Beckoned by the bookcases — filled with so many books, they must be purged every two or three years — I got up and walked in my bare feet across the coral-peach handmade carpet from Afghanistan, the one I ordered two years ago thinking it might inspire my imagination. The wool was soft, cloud-like. As I stood in front of the bookshelf, searching the titles, I asked for a word that would pull me out of the metaphorical mud that had brought my work to a standstill. As soon as I pulled out a book, the landline began to ring downstairs, so I put it back on the shelf and ran down the steps, holding the handrail. The telephone screen told me it was an official call, and when I answered, a woman on the other end said, "We have approved coverage of the new medication for treatment of your osteoporosis. Your doctor will be in touch to schedule you for the monthly shots."

"That's wonderful news. Thank you," I said.

When they were first ordered, my husband and I discovered that the shots were so expensive, we'd never be able to afford them, so this was a miracle. I hesitated just a moment then hung up the receiver, walked across the bedroom to the window, and glanced out at the trees again. They looked so different from the second floor. Thicker, filled with life, unlike my frail bones. *Hmmm…injections. The trees get heavy with life, and I have to take shots to keep my skeleton intact.* I walked back up to the third floor to my desk and started searching for my online patient portal. Here it was, the file with test results of my bone scan, performed six months ago by the Osteoporosis Testing Facility, just before the season turned from fall to winter. It was the second day in October, and I was packing for my trip to southern France for the pilgrimage to Mary Magdalene's grotto. The leaves were turning from green to orange and gold.

I studied the chart, reading the numbers aloud.

"Left Hip: Normal score= 3.7. My score= -1.6.

Spine: Normal score= 3.4. My score= -1.0."

I did the math, saying to myself, "That was -2.1 for my hip and -2.4 for my spine."

More than two points shy on each measurement. The pictures of my bones were hazy, eerie. They looked thin, more like sponge than bone. My doctor had warned me that I was at risk of breaking my hip, spine, or femur. I knew the danger of traveling to a foreign country with such a diagnosis, but something about the pilgrimage had drawn me forward. *Was it the knowledge that I would see the site in the Alps where Mary lived until she was my age? Was I lured by the idea of storytelling?*

Remembering the climb up the mountain I'd made a few months earlier, I thought about the risk I'd taken, walking into the shadowy grotto, descending the water-covered rock steps into the womb of the damp cave to pray at Mary's statue. Candles had lined the floor of the cave, giving me just enough light to walk back up the stairs. *Looking back,* I wondered, *why had I taken such a chance? What compelled me to walk in the darkness? What if I had fallen and broken a bone? How would I get home?* I was not usually given to gambling with my money or health, but I couldn't resist the pull to learn more of the legend about the woman carrying Jesus' story across the sea in a rudderless boat. *Hmm,* I thought. *Not unlike me, flying across the ocean with weak bones.*

All my life I had been in search of more. More information. More of the story. Now, I wanted to know additional information about my medical condition. I pulled up the most recent laboratory tests run by my new doctor, a specialist in osteoporosis, to search for clues that might explain my bone loss. The blood work had been done months after I returned from the trip, in late April, just as the trees had begun to flash signs of changing color. Eight tests in all. To my surprise, not one revealed a vitamin deficiency, nor any other reason for the poor health of my bones. No evidence of a coexisting condition that contributed to the disease.

How could that be? I wondered. *Nothing to suggest how or why my skeleton had become so weak.* "How can such extensive blood work leave me with more questions?" I asked the room.

Something caught my eye, and I leaned over the desk to look out the window. Three deer were walking across the field, moving slowly toward the edge of the woods where the trees stood, incandescent, luminous, leaves seeming to wave them deeper into the green forest. I wondered, *What do the trees know about surviving a long life, even a cold, wet winter season, until spring arrives? How could they have known they'd survive long enough to host a new season of animals and humans? What did they know about building tissue that my body didn't seem to be able to grasp? Maybe it was a deep understanding held in the heart of the trunks.*

I sat back down at the computer and did a quick search for trees and learned they are sustained through an unseen process by which the inner tissue, known as the phloem, transports sap to the roots. Photosynthesis, a complex biological method that cannot be seen by the naked eye. It was a logic understood only by the trees. *Mysterious. Magical. Beautiful. And invisible, much like the deterioration of my bones.* This was also the nature of story that had both called to and confounded me. Daring me to search for more, yet yielding so little information. Like the trees, the story had endured because of an unseen system of subsistence. *What kind of magic had kept my precious intergenerational stories alive?*

I remembered one day the previous summer, when my husband and I walked to the edge of the forest, stopping at a large oak tree. "Here," I said. "This is where I'll build it." For days, we gathered up large tree limbs from the ground and built a circle around the tree.

"It's awfully close to the park. Aren't you worried that someone will be tempted to break it apart?" he asked.

"No, I'm not worried. I don't think anyone will touch it," I replied.

We continued to work, gathering up fallen tree limbs and fashioning a fairly large circle, placing a small wooden cross in the center. I stood inside and wrapped my arms around the tree — not caring if anyone saw me. "This will be my special tree where I'll come to remember and honor my ancestors." We had returned to the prayer circle weekly and, six months later, one day before Christmas, we went back to check on it. I stood inside the circle of limbs. It had not been touched. No one had tried to move or rearrange the limbs. Maybe, I thought, because the circle was charged with a sacred energy that others felt but did not see. I would never forget that day.

I put the lab reports and bone scans back down on the desk, put on my shoes and a light jacket, and walked outside to the tree and my prayer circle again that morning. As I stood inside the circle, I felt the change in the air, now filled with moisture that, when it hit my skin, transported me back to the St. Baume Grotto, and the damp, moist cave in the mountain that held the memory of my spiritual sister, Mary Magdalene. I listened for the sound of trees moving in the wind, ran my fingers across the bark, and asked the tree, "How can I learn what you know?"

I considered my own life, filled with a kind of unheard rhythm leading me through the years. Perhaps my life had been following a pattern that was unknowable. Then, in response to a silent summons, I walked deeper into the wilderness and stepped into the shade of larger trees. It was here, standing in the darkness, in the stillness where I began to see. The changing of the trees each year had enchanted me, lulling me in the same way the forest in southern France had. They were both holding me inside a story that had sustained itself over the years. Maybe, like the system that provided nourishment to the trees, the process of carrying stories could never really be known. I had been able to compose a few pieces about my life, but I knew I would never see enough springs to find the whole narrative of my family, nor to understand the complex procedure that had kept the story alive. All I could do was cast the seeds for the next story carrier in the family to pick up the tale and follow it.

Then it occurred to me that there was a connection between never knowing the end of the story and my medical condition. Could it be that by remaining elusive, the story survived generation after generation? That by remaining untold, it would have the power to draw a new family member inward to their own path in search of the story. *Perhaps I could also learn to accept living without complete resolution. Without knowing the full story.*

I walked back out of the woods and returned to the house, where I opened my medical files once more. I called up copies of my bone scans and lab results and printed them out so I could read over them more closely. They read differently to me now. More than a list of values and numbers, more than frail images mapping out the presence of a serious medical condition. They painted a picture of a body that had borne stories, even those I hadn't heard or known. Ancestral stories carried in my family for generations. Stories that were held in the land, in the sky, the trees, the soil. I held the copies up again seeing, for the first time, what exactly they were. They were evidence. Proof of my membership in a tribe of story carriers and my passport to the imaginary realm where more stories lived. This was the reason my bones had opened up like a sponge; they were providing tiny hollow spaces for stories to soak in and remain until they were ready to be told.

I decided to keep my appointment with the specialist in a few weeks and allow her to give me the shots prescribed for my condition. I'd release my insistence on being given a prognosis. I'd learn to stand in the mystery of not-knowingness, and like the trees in the forest that invited the deer into their home, I would open my heart up to stories, nurturing and carrying them in my bones, my body. My story had never been disappeared. I had been carrying the story of my family all along. I only had to allow it to unfold, to teach me the language to speak it into being. This, I thought, was the magical process of becoming a story carrier.

Acknowledgements

It is always a gamble when a writer sets out to follow the thread of a story that resists being woven into a larger narrative, and I am grateful for those who encouraged me through the process of bringing this one together. My list is divided into two groups: the living and the dead. All helped me get to a story, which had been hidden in my family for years.

My mother taught me how a woman can grow and change across her lifetime, how she can transform from a young woman struggling to handle young children and blossom into a wise, loving elder who supports her adult daughter, especially as she tries to navigate a system that undervalues women and mothers. My grandmother taught me how to "walk the Miss America walk," balancing a book on my head, and to claim my space in the world with dignity. My great grandmother, Vina, who I never met, taught me that those who depart this life are still with us, helping us carry stories until we are able to bring them into language. She showed me how an ancestor can deliver a shimmering memory in the form of a dream, guiding us to the stories that have been hidden. My older sister, Jeanie, who cared for me as an infant, taught me how to carry a story in the soul before it can be articulated in a story.

I could never have told this story without the support and love of a community of women who journeyed with me on a pilgrimage to southern France, led by Veronique Flayol, to the grotto where Mary Magdalene spent her final years. I am grateful for the example of Mary Magdalene, who courageously carried the biggest story in Christian history, that of the resurrection, in spite of the Roman church's effort to silence her, and for her persistence to survive as a story carrier.

The will always be grateful for the deep listening and witnessing provided by my writing group, including Mary Aebischer, Devany Ledrew, Sharon Wilson, Debbie Hackett, and Mary Margaret McNaughton, who carried me through three years as I struggled with revisions to my manuscript, providing in-depth, meaningful feedback. I am grateful for the intuitive gifts of my writing coach and publisher, Brooke Adams Law, whose gift for seeing and hearing my story before it was fully told, helped me to feel the presence of the tale and trust myself to bring it into being.

Finally, and, perhaps most importantly, I want to acknowledge the love and support I received from my husband, who spent many evenings parked in front of the television watching re-runs of Law and Order, watering my flowers, and working jigsaw puzzles while I wrote into the wee hours of the morning. He traveled with me to Texas, to find family graves, helped me locate documents, and spent hours holding my hand. His endearing love lights up the pages of this book and I will forever consider him to be my co-writer.

Recommendations for Further Reading

Vicuna, Cecilia. "The Disappeared." 2021. *Poets.Org.*
This poem greatly inspired me on my writing journey.
Introduction
Bolen, Jean Shinoda. *Goddesses in Everywoman: Powerful Archetypes in Women's Lives.* Harper, 1984.
Bolen, Jean Shinoda. *Gods in Everyman: Archetypes That Shape Men's Lives.* Harper, 1989.
Butler, Robert Olen. *From Where You Dream: The Process of Writing Fiction.* Grove Press, 2005.
Estés, Clarissa Pinkola. *Women Who Run with the Wolves: Myths and Stories of the Wild Woman Archetype.* Ballantine Books, 1992.
Chapter 3
Williamson, G.R. *The El Paso Salt War: The Bloody Texas Saga of 1877.* Indian Head Publishing, 2023.
Chapter 4
"Nuestra Senora Del Pilar (Our Lady of the Pillar)." *Catholic News Agency.*
Stevenson, Robert Louis. *The Lantern Bearers and Other Essays.* Cooper Square Press, 1999.
Chapter 7
"Abortion Control Act, 1982: Casey Vs. Planned Parenthood: Ruling, Controversy & Legacy." *History.com*, A&E Television

Networks, 24 June 2022.

"Freind Backs Off From Rape Statement." *The Morning Call*, 30 Mar. 1988.

"With Some 'Imprecise' Remarks on Sexual Assault, State Rep. Stephen Freind Has Ignited the Anger of Educators, Feminists and Physicians Rape and Rhetoric." *The Morning Call*, 5 April 1988.

Chapter 12

Dickinson, Emily. *The Complete Poems of Emily Dickinson*. Little, Brown and Company, 1976.

"Global Mystics Certification with Andrew Harvey & Mirabai Starr." *The Shift Network*, 2021.

Watterson, Meggan. *Reveal: A Sacred Manual for Getting Spiritually Naked*. Hay House, Inc., 2013.

Chapter 14

Erickson, Lori. "Terlingua Cemetery in Texas: A Destination Graveyard." *Spiritual Travels,* 23 Aug. 2021.

Chapter 15

Rich, Adrienne. *Of Woman Born: Motherhood as Experience and Institution*. W.W. Norton & Co, 1995.

Chapter 16

"Welcome to Sainte-Baume." *Sanctuaire-de-la-Sainte-Baume*.

Chapter 17

Moore, Kate. "The American History of Silencing Women through Psychiatry." *Time Magazine*, 22 June 2021.

Prichard, James Cowles. *A Treatise on Insanity and Other Disorders Affecting the Mind*. Haswell, Barrington, 1835.

About the Author

Jane Hollinger Clark is a retired college teacher of composition, literature, and journalism, who worked for a major northeastern university and a small, private liberal arts college. She was employed by the National Writing Project in Berkeley, CA, and directed a local branch of the NWP at PSU, Harrisburg. Before entering academia, she spent years chasing legislative stories as a journalist for the Associated Press and Radio Pennsylvania. She now devotes her time to facilitating writing workshops for her church, gardening, and traveling with her husband in their home near the Appalachian Forest in Pennsylvania.